GAELIC WITHOUT GROANS

D1331286

GAELIC
Without Groans

JOHN MACKECHNIE, M.A.

OLIVER & BOYD
EDINBURGH

OLIVER & BOYD
Croythorn House
23 Ravelston Terrace
Edinburgh EH4 3TJ

A Division of Longman Group Ltd.

First published (Eneas Mackay) . . 1934
Second revised edition . . . 1962
Reprinted . 1963, 1965, 1966, 1969, 1970, 1971
Third edition . . . . . ·1974
Reprinted 1977

© 1962, 1974 (except for Vocabulary Check
List) J. Mackechnie. Vocabulary Check List
© 1974 Oliver & Boyd. All rights reserved.
No part of this publication may be reproduced,
stored in a retrieval system, or transmitted,
in any form or by any means electronic, mechanical
photocopying, recording or otherwise, without
prior permission of the copyright owners and
publisher. All enquiries should be addressed to
the publisher in the first instance.

0 05 002862 6

Printed in Hong Kong by
Commonwealth Printing Press Ltd

PREFACE

The purpose of this little book is to help the reader to get a working knowledge of Gaelic in the shortest possible time. Many people both inside and outside of Scotland, would like to learn Gaelic, yet they are deterred by the thought of having to wade through a grammar-book. One can sympathise with them, for grammar is dry-as-dust to the ordinary man, but language is a living thing and, as far as possible, should be taught in a live, human way. For this reason the lessons have been written in a simple conversational style, and even, on occasion, the Doric has been introduced.

This book is in the nature of a pioneer work and will, therefore, have its critics. No doubt, matter and methods could be improved in many ways, but there is no suggestion that there is anything of finality in this work. Little serious effort has yet been made to present Gaelic in a popular and attractive fashion, such as has been done in the case of French, German and other Continental languages. If Gaelic is to survive at all, a beginning along these lines must be made somehow, somewhere and by someone. Therefore, if this little volume, as well as bringing the language within the reach of the man in the street, will also stimulate others to improve on its methods and thus give further impetus to the Gaelic movement in Scotland and elsewhere, it will have achieved its purpose.

Approximate phonetic equivalents have been used instead of the International Phonetic Alphabet, simply because the latter, unfortunately, is unlikely to be known to the majority of the readers for whom these lessons have been designed.

The reader will find the proverbs at the beginning of the lessons difficult—wise words are usually hard to grasp—but they show something of the Gaelic speaker's outlook on things, and in time the reader will, we hope, be quoting them with gusto.

In bringing out this second edition of the work we have made full use of the many suggestions made by various critics, helpful and otherwise, about the first edition. To all who have contributed to the improvement of the work we give our sincere thanks.

JOHN MACKECHNIE.

INTRODUCTION

The few short notes which follow will be of help to the reader in pronouncing Gaelic.

If you look at a page of Gaelic, you will notice little marks such as ` and ´ above some of the words. These are accent-marks, but do not let your experience of French frighten you here. They are very easy in Gaelic. Thus:—

ó is sounded like **o** in the English word tone.
ò is sounded like **o** in the English word job.
é is sounded like **a** in the English word say.
è is sounded like **e** in the English word get.

Now for **a**, **u** and **i**: when these get a long sound, we write them thus **à**, **ù**, and **ì**, and sound them as in the English words dam, doom and deem. Note that **ì** sounds like the English **ee** and **ù** like the English **oo**.

S before **e** or **i** in a Gaelic word is pronounced like **sh** in the English word show.

In those lessons the word which shows the pronunciation of the Gaelic is always enclosed in brackets, and a bar put over the syllable which is stressed, thus: **còta** (kāw-ta); when the stressed syllable contains two vowels, the bar is put over each vowel, e.g., ōō. Note, too, that **tsh** is pronounced like **tch** in the English word catch, while **ch** is pronounced like **ch** in the English word loch.

Lesson No. 1

Obair là — tòiseachadh. *A day's work — getting started.*

It is really not such a hard thing to learn Gaelic as some folk think. It is quite true, I admit, that many people have spent years trying to master this beautiful old tongue and have failed. But why? Simply because they have tried to learn the language from a grammar-book and grammar is an abomination to 99 people out of 100.

Gaelic presents fewer difficulties of pronunciation than most modern languages, and so, instead of inflicting upon the student a table of sounds, I have chosen rather to give the approximate sound of the words by means of English symbols. A very little practice and the spelling will be found to be quite simple.

In Gaelic the verb (or doing or telling word) always comes at the beginning of the sentence. For instance, the word **tha** which means **is** or **are**, is used as follows:—**tha mi**, I am; **tha sinn**, we are; **tha Seumas**, James is. Here is the present form (or tense) of the verb:—

tha mi (ha mēē), I am.
tha thu (ha ōō), thou art or you are.
tha e (ha eh—e as in get), he is.
tha i (ha ee—ee as in feet), she is.
tha sinn (ha shēēng), we are.
tha sibh (ha shiv), you are.
tha iad (ha ēē-ut), they are.

9

The past tense is equally simple: instead of **tha** put **bha** (va) which means was or were into the above table. Thus:—

bha mi (va mēē), I was.
bha thu (va ōō), thou wast, etc.

Further examples of the use of those forms are:—**tha mi fuar** (fōō-ar), I am cold; **bha thu fliuch** (flooch—**ch** sounded as in loch), you were wet; **tha Seumas beag** (bake), James is small; **tha an là fuar,** the day is cold. In this last example, notice that the word **an** stands for the; **là** itself means day or a day, there being no word for a in Gaelic. The adjective (or describing word) in Gaelic usually follows the noun (or name word), e.g., **là fuar,** a cold day.

The little word **aig** (ek), which means at, is one of the most useful in Gaelic. For instance, where in English we say "I have a dog", we say in Gaelic that a dog is "at me". So again, "James has a knife" becomes in Gaelic, "a knife is at James", i.e., **tha sgian** (skēē-an) **aig Seumas**. "He has a coat", i.e., "a coat is at him" becomes **tha còta aige**. Notice how **aig** and **e** are combined into one word, becoming **aige** which means "at him". In the same way **mi**, **tu**, etc., are joined with **aig** to form one word, although slight changes in the forms have crept in during the course of time. Thus:—

aig+**mi** becomes **agam** (ākum), at me.
aig+**tu** becomes **agad** (ākut), at you.
aig+**sinn** becomes **againn** (āking), at us.
aig+**sibh** becomes **agaibh** (ākiv), at you.

The form **aice** (ēchk-eh) is used for **aig**+**i**, and **aca** (āch-ka) for **aig**+**iad**. The following examples will make the above clear:—

"I have a dog", i.e., a dog is at me, **tha cù agam**.
"You have a horse", i.e., a horse is at you, **tha each** (ech— ch as in loch) **agad**.

"You (plural) have bread", i.e., bread is at you, **tha aran agaibh.**

"They have cheese", i.e., cheese is at them, **tha càise** (kā-sheh) **aca.**

Likewise "I had a dog" becomes a dog was at me, i.e., **bha cù agam.** "You had a purse" becomes a purse was at you, i.e., **bha sporan** (spōr-un) **agad,** etc. In Gaelic everything is a he or a she: there are no its, e.g., a ship is a she, so is a train, a river, while fire, iron, a day, etc., are counted as he's or males. Later on in those lessons you will learn which are "he" words and which are "she".

VOCABULARY

ach (ch as in loch), but.

aig (ek), at.

air, on.

a nis (a nēēsh), now.

anns an, in the.

aran (ārran), bread.

a' ruith (a rōō-eech—ch as in loch), running.

beag (bake), little, small.

blàth (blaa), warm.

bochd (boch-k), poor.

bradan (brāt-an), salmon.

cat (kah-t), a cat.

còta (kāw-ta), a coat.

cù (koo), a dog.

dorus (dōrr-is), a door.

dubh (doo—pronounced very short), black.

duine (dōōn-ye), a man.

dùn (doon pronounced very long), a castle, hillock.

each (ech—ch as in loch), a horse.

fliuch (floo-ch), wet.

fuar (foo-ar), cold.

glas, gray.

là, a day.

loch (lo-ch), a loch.

long (lō-ng), a ship, boat.

mac (māch-k), son.

Màiri (mā-ree), Mary.

mór (mō-r), great, big.

òg (awk), young.

rìgh (ree), a king.

Seumas (Shāy-mus), James

sgian (skēē-an), a knife.

sgoil (skol), a school.

sporan (spōr-un), a purse.

teine (tshāing-eh), a fire.

tigh (ta-ee—pronounced very short), house.

tioram (tshīr-ram), dry.

tobar (tōpe-ur), a well.

uisge (ōōshk-eh), water.

TRANSLATE THE FOLLOWING INTO ENGLISH

(1) An cat ; an cù ; an dorus ; an tobar; an loch ; an sgian

(2) Cat glas ; cù dubh ; dorus mór ; tobar beag ; duine bochd.

(3) Tha an cat dubh ; tha an cù mór ; tha an dorus beag ; bha an duine òg ; bha an còta fliuch, ach tha e a nis tioram.

(4) Aig an dùn ; air an loch ; aig an tobar, agus aig an teine.

(5) Tha Seumas air an loch, ach tha Màiri aig an dùn ; bha còta air Seumas ; tha uisge anns an tobar.

(6) Bha Seumas a' ruith.

(7) Tha each agam ; bha sgian agad ; bha long aige ; tha cat aca ; bha teine aca air an dùn ; tha mac aice ; bha bradan agaibh.

TRANSLATE INTO GAELIC

(1) a salmon; a dog; a cat; a ship.

(2) the man; the ship; the fire; the loch; the well.

(3) the loch is big; the ship was small; the man is cold; the fire was warm; the knife is black.

(4) at the door; on the loch; at the hillock.

(5) the dog was at the loch; the man is at the door; Mary was in the school; the dog was running.

(6) I have a knife; you have a ship; he has a house; we have a fire now; they have a king; you (pl.) have a purse.

SOLUTION OF LESSON 1

(1) Bradan ; cù ; cat ; long.

(2) An duine ; an long ; an teine ; an loch ; an tobar.

(3) Tha an loch mór ; bha an long beag ; tha an duine fuar ; bha an teine blàth ; tha an sgian dubh.

(4) Aig an dorus ; air an loch ; aig an dùn.

(5) Bha an cù aig an loch ; tha an duine aig an dorus ; bha Màiri anns an sgoil ; bha an cù a' ruith.

(6) Tha sgian agam ; tha long agad ; tha tigh aige ; tha teine againn a nis ; tha rìgh aca ; tha sporan agaibh.

Lesson No. 2

Ceilidh gràdh gràin. *Love hides (even) disgust.*

We have seen that a plain statement like "he is cold" is translated by **tha e fuar**. Suppose, now, we wish to put this in the form of a question, we begin with a little word **an** (written **am** before **b**, **f**, **m**, **p**) and instead of using **tha** we use **bheil** (vale—pronounced very short), which is the question form of **tha**. Thus, **am bheil e fuar ?** "is he cold ?"; **am bheil thu fliuch ?** "are you wet ?" ; and **am bheil an tobar tioram ?** "is the well dry ?"

Again, if you want to say "he is not cold", you put **cha** for the "not" at the beginning of the phrase, and the **bheil** is shortened to **-eil** (ale). Thus, **cha n-eil** (nyale) **e fuar**, "he is not cold"; the **n** before **-eil** merely helps to make the sound glide smoothly. So too, **cha n-eil thu fliuch**, "you are not wet", etc. Gaelic speakers are just like other folk when answering questions, the shorter the reply the sooner said, and so they would simply say, **cha n-eil**, the **thu fuar, fliuch**, etc., being missed out.

But there may be some doubt in our minds when we ask a question. For instance, I may say, "are you not cold ?" and this is translated by **nach 'eil thu fuar ?** where **nach** both asks a question and shows that there is some doubt about the answer. Well, the answer would be either **tha (mi fuar)**, "I am cold", or **cha n-eil (mi fuar)**, "I am not cold", the **mi fuar** being usually left out. **Nach 'eil an tobar tioram ?** "is the well not dry ?" is answered either by **tha**, "it is", or **cha n-eil**, "it isn't".

In past time, when we ask a question or deny anything, we use **robh** (ro) instead of **bha**. Thus **an robh thu fuar ?** means "were you cold ?" The answer is either **bha**, "I was",

14

or **cha robh**, "I was not"—the **mi fuar** as usual being missed out.

In Lesson No. 1 we saw that the word **aig** was very useful, and now we add other examples of its usefulness.

In English we say, "James is fishing" for "James is a' fishing" or "James is at fishing". This is turned into Gaelic by **tha Seumas ag iasgach** (ēē-us-gach), or in the past, **bha Seumas ag iasgach**. The word **ag** here is just another form of **aig** which, as has already been shown means "at". Again "he is saying . . ." becomes **tha e ag ràdh** (a krā) . . . and "he was saying . . ." becomes **bha e ag ràdh** . . . For ease in speaking, **ag** is usually shortened to **a'** except before a vowel, **c** or **g**, and the word **ràdh** which means "saying". Thus we have **tha e a' snàmh**, "he is swimming", but on the other hand, **bha e ag òl**, "he was drinking".

When we wish to say how a thing is done, we put **gu** (goo) in front of the adjective (or describing word); thus **luath** (lōō-a), "quick", **gu luath**, "quickly", e.g., **bha e a' ruith gu luath**, "he was running quickly".

Gu placed thus before an adjective has the same meaning as the English ending "-ly". **Gu'n** (gōōn), (**gu'm** before **b**, **f**, **m**, **p**) when used before a verb (or doing word), means "that", e.g., **gu'm bheil mi, thu**, etc., "that I am, you are", etc.; so, too, **gu'n robh mi, thu**, etc., "that I was, that you were", etc. For example, **tha e ag ràdh gu'n robh Seumas ag iasgach** means "he is saying that James was fishing".

An so means "here" and **an sin** means "there"; **an duine so** means literally "the man here", i.e., "this man", and **an duine sin** "the man there", i.e., "that man". So also **an tigh so** means "this house" and **am baile sin**, "that town".

VOCABULARY

a' dol (dol), going, a' going.
a' fàs, growing.
ag cadal (katl), sleeping.

ag coiseachd (kāwsh-achk), walking.
ag creidsinn (krītsh-ing), believing.
a' seinn (shāy-ing), singing.
a' snàmh (snā-v), swimming.
a' suidhe (sōō-ee), sitting.
ag òl (āwl), drinking.
agus (āgh-us—"gh" as in "ugh"), and : also sometimes **is**.
am mac, the son (**an** becoming **am** before **m**).
an dé (un jāy), yesterday.
an diugh (un jōō—pronounced very short), to-day.
an nochd (un nāwch-k), to-night.
an raoir (un rēr), yesterday evening, last night.
breac (brech-k), a trout.
cinnteach (kēēn-tshach), certain, sure.
có ?, who ?
dachaidh (dāch-eh), home.
deagh (jo), good, excellent.
mall (mā-ool), slow.
seo or **so** (shāw—pronounced very short), this.
spiorad (spēē-rut), a spirit; **spioradan** (spēē-rut-un), spirits, intoxicating liquors.
tannasg (tā-nask), a ghost, spirit; **tannasgan** (tā-nask-un), ghosts.
tighinn (tshee-ing), coming.
tigh-òsda (āws-ty), an inn.

TRANSLATE INTO ENGLISH

(1) Am bheil an là fuar ? Nach 'eil an duine air an dùn ?
Cha n-eil, ach tha e air an loch. An robh thu a'
dol dachaidh ? Có bha ag òl an dé ? Nach 'eil am
mac òg a' fàs mór ? Tha, gu cinnteach. Am bheil
an cù luath ? Cha n-eil, tha e mall.

(2) Bha e ag ràdh gu'n robh an là fuar. Nach robh thu ag
ràdh gu'n robh thu a' dol dachaidh ? Am bheil iad

ag ràdh gu'm bheil cù aca ? Cha n-eil, ach tha e
ag ràdh gu'n robh each aige.

(3) Bha iad a' snàmh anns an loch an raoir. Nach robh
e ag coiseachd an dé ? Cha robh, bha e ag cadal.
Có tha a' seinn anns an dorus ?* Tha duine bochd,
fliuch, fuar. Tha mi ag creidsinn gu'm bheil an
là fuar.

* Note.—**anns an dorus** means "at the door".

TRANSLATE INTO GAELIC

Is Mary at (use **anns an***) the door ? No, she is at the
well. Who is sitting on the hillock ? James. Were you not
fishing on the loch to-day ? I was not. I was sitting in the
house. Who was saying that he was going home last night ?
He says that you are singing slowly. Had you a salmon ?
No, I had not, but I had a trout. We were walking at the
loch yesterday. Was it not wet, and were you not cold ?
We were cold and wet. I am certain that the son is coming
home to-day.

SOLUTION OF LESSON 2

**Am bheil Màiri anns an dorus ? Cha n-eil. Tha i aig
an tobar. Có tha a' suidhe air an dùn ? Seumas (or,
tha Seumas). Nach robh thu ag iasgach air an loch an
diugh ? Cha robh. Bha mi a' suidhe anns an tigh.
Có bha ag ràdh gu'n robh e a' dol dachaidh an raoir ?
Tha e ag ràdh gu'm bheil thu a' seinn gu mall. An robh
bradan agad ? Cha robh, ach bha breac agam. Bha
sinn ag coiseachd aig an loch an dé. Nach robh e fliuch
agus nach robh sibh fuar ? Bha sinn fuar agus fliuch.
Tha mi cinnteach gu'm bheil am mac a' tighinn
dachaidh an diugh.**

* Cf. Lesson 17.

Lesson No. 3

Na tog mi gus an tuit mi.   *Don't lift me up till I fall.*

Consider the words, "peasant" and "pheasant": in both sound and spelling they are almost alike. The only difference is that by putting **h** after **p** we altered the **p** sound to an **f** sound, as in "pheasant".

Now, the custom of putting an **h** after certain letters to alter their sound is very common in Gaelic, and is called "aspiration". The chief letters that are aspirated are, **b, c, d, f, g, m, p, s, t,** and the following little table will show at a glance what changes take place in their sounds.

ch—sound as **ch** in loch.

ph—sound as **ph** in pheasant.

sh—sound as **hyawl** before **-eo-**.*

th—sound as **h** in hat.

bh and **mh**—sound as **v** in vat.

dh and **gh**—sound as **gh** in ugh! or like **ch** deep down in the throat. But when **dh** or **gh** come before **e** or **i**, they sound like **y** in yellow.

fh has no sound at all; thus a word like **fhill** would sound just the same as "eel". Only three words break this rule; these are—**fhéin** (hāy-nn), self; **fhuair** (hōō-ar), got or found, and **fhathast** (hā-ast), yet, where **fh** is sounded as **h**.

The music of the Gaelic speech is due in large measure to the use of aspiration, which causes sounds to glide into one another. Let us take an example of how aspiration works.

Tog! (tōke) is the Gaelic word for " lift !" e.g., **tog an sgian!** "lift the knife !" Now, to put this into past time, simply aspirate the **t** of **tog**, thus, **thog** (hōke) **e an sgian**, "he lifted the knife".

---

* There is no sound like this in English. Elsewhere **sh** is sounded as **h** in hat.

Other examples are:—**bris** ! (breesh), break !; e.g., **bris an copan** ! "break the cup !" Hence **bhris i an copan**, "she broke the cup". **Seas** ! (shāyss), "stand !" Hence **sheas** (hāyss) **iad aig an tigh**, "they stood at the house".

Here is another place where we use aspiration. The Gaelic word for "my" (or "mine") is **mo** (mo as in motor) and it causes the word that comes after it to be aspirated. For instance, **bàta** means "a boat", and **mo bhàta** means "my boat". Likewise **do bhàta** (do as in don't) means "thy (or your) boat", and **a bhàta**, "his boat". But, on the other hand, there is no aspiration with **a bàta**, "her boat", or, in other words, **a** with aspiration means "his", but without, it means "her".

Ar bàta, "our boat"; **bhur bàta**, "your boat"; **am bàta**, "their boat"; **an gual** (gōō-ul), "their coal". Notice that **an** meaning "their" becomes **am** before **b, f, m, p**. The same holds good for **an** meaning "the", e.g., **an long**, "the ship"; but **am bòrd**, "the table".

Further examples are:—**mo chù**, "my dog"; **m' uan** (ōō-an), "my lamb"; **do bhrochan**, "thy (or your) porridge"; **d' aran**, "thy bread"; **a phìob**, "his pipe"; **a fhìon**, "his wine", but **a fìon**, "her wine"; **ar Seumas**, "our James"; **ar n'athair** (a-ir), "our father"; **bhur tìr** (voor tsheer), "your land"; **bhur n'àite** (ātchy), "your place"; **an dorus**, "their door"; **am fìon**, "their wine". Before a vowel **mo** and **do** drop **o**, hence the apostrophe, while **ar** and **bhur** are followed by an **n**. Again, instead of writing **d' aran** for "thy bread" we generally write **t' aran**, i.e., **t'** instead of **d'**. So also before all words beginning with a vowel, or words beginning with **f** followed by a vowel this **d** meaning "thy" usually becomes **t**.

VOCABULARY

a, who, which, that.

an seo, or, **an so** (un-shāw—pronounced very short), here.

athair (ā-ir), father.

anns an abhainn (ā-ving), in the burn or stream.

balach, boy.

bròg (brāw-k), a shoe or boot.

brògan (brāw-kin), shoes.

buail! (bōō-ile), strike!

bràthair (brā-ir), a brother.

caraid (cār-itsh), a friend.

ceann (kyā-oon), a head.

cìr (keer), a comb.

copan (kōpan), a cup.

creutair (krāy-tur), a creature.

caill! (kȳ-ile), lose!

dùin! (dōō-in), shut!

duais (dōō-aish), reward, pay, prize.

fearg (fēr-uk), anger, wrath.

gunna (gōōn-a), a gun.

làmh (lāāv), a hand; **làmhan** (lāvin), hands.

leabhar (lyō-ur), a book.

màthair (mā-ir), a mother.

mol! (mawl—pronounced very short), praise!

peann (pyā-oon), a pen.

piuthar (pyōō-ar), a sister.

saighdear (sy-tshir), a soldier.

sàil (sā-il), a heel.

sin (sheeng—pronounced very short), that.

sluagh (slōō-ah), people, a crowd.

sùil (sōō-il), an eye.

tilg! (tshēēl-ik), throw!

tinn (tshēēng), sick, ill.

tuit! (tōō-itsh), fall!

uinneag (ōō-ing-ak), a window.

ùrlar (ōōr-lar), a floor.

TRANSLATE INTO ENGLISH

Mo bhròg; ar brògan; a mhàthair; do cheann; a cìr; bhur sùilean; a shàil; am fearg; an làmhan.

Tog am peann. Thog mi a pheann. Buail an duine! Bhuail iad an duine. Thilg e copan air an ùrlar. Sheas saighdear aig mo thigh. Thuit am balach anns an abhainn. Dhùin mo bhràthair an uinneag. Bha m' athair ag iasgach anns an loch agus fhuair e breac. An robh a phiuthar anns an sgoil an diugh? Cha robh. Bha i tinn. Mhol e am mac a fhuair duais aig an sgoil. Nach 'eil mo leabhar agad? Cha n-eil, ach tha e aig mo charaid a bha an so an dé. Thog e mo chat agus thilg e an creutair bochd anns an loch.

TRANSLATE INTO GAELIC

My pen; our hands; our lamb; his sister; your comb; his trout; their friend; our cat; her heel; your door; their father. Are my shoes here? No! Your pipe is on the floor. Our people are in the land. The soldier lost his gun. The little boy fell in the well. We found your lamb at the hillock to-day. Your porridge is cold. His dog found my lamb. He says that their friend has my book (my book is at their friend).

SOLUTION OF LESSON No. 3

Mo pheann; ar làmhan; ar n-uan; a phiuthar; do chìr; a bhreac; an caraid; ar cat; a sàil; do dhorus; an athair. Am bheil mo bhrògan an so? Cha n-eil. Tha do phìob air an ùrlar. Tha ar sluagh anns an tìr. Chaill an saighdear a ghunna. Thuit am balach beag anns an tobar. Fhuair sinn d' uan aig an dùn an diugh. Tha do bhrochan fuar. Fhuair a chù m' uan. Tha e ag ràdh gu'm bheil mo leabhar aig an caraid.

Lesson No. 4

Tigh gun chù gun chat gun leanabh beag, tigh gun
ghean gun ghàire. *A house without a dog, a cat, or
a little child is one without affection or merriment.*

We saw in the last lesson that to show past tense we aspirated
(i.e., put an **h** after) the first letter of the doing-word or verb.

Thus **tog an sgian!** "lift the knife!" becomes **thog e an
sgian,** "he lifted the knife". This aspiration is caused by a
little word **do*** which used to be put before the verb to show
past time, e.g., **do thog e an sgian,** "he lifted the knife".

Suppose, however, that the verb begins with a vowel, as
òl! "drink!" or **f** followed by a vowel, as **fan!** "stay!" Now,
we cannot aspirate a vowel, and **f** itself, when aspirated (**fh**)
is, as we know, silent. To get over our difficulty we put **dh'**
in front of such words. This **dh'** is just a broken-down form
of the **do** mentioned above. Hence:—

dh'òl mi an leann (ghōl mēē un lyā-oon), I drank the beer.
dh'fhan i aig baile (ghan ēē ek bāl-y), she stayed at home.
dh'innis e sgeul (yēē-ish eh skāy-l), he told a tale.
dh'fhosgail e an dorus (ghōskal eh un dōrris), he opened
the door.

But note carefully the following :—

fhreagair e mo cheisd (rāy-kir eh mo chāy-sht), he answered
my question.
fhliuch sinn ar casan (lōōch shēēng ur kāsn), we wet our
feet.

There is no **dh** in those words because **f** in **freagair** and
in **fliuch** is not followed by a vowel.

* Cf. Lesson 17.

When we wish to ask a question, or to deny anything that has been said in the past, we must in every case restore **do** before the verb, even when there is already **dh'**.

Thus:—**An do thuit** (hōō-itsh) **e anns an abhainn ?** did he fall into the river ?; **nach do thuit e anns an abhainn ?** did he not fall into the river ?

To which the answer is:—**Cha do thuit** (**e anns an abhainn**), he did not fall (into the river), i.e., No ! or, **Thuit** (**e anns an abhainn**), he did (fall into the river), i.e., Yes !

Cha do thuit and **Thuit** are shortened forms like the English "I did" and "I didn't"—the rest of the sentence being generally omitted.

Note carefully that there is no single word in Gaelic for giving the answers "Yes", or "No".

Further examples:—

An do dh'òl e am bainne ? (bān-yeh). Did he drink the milk ?

Nach do dh'òl e am bainne ? Did he not drink the milk ?

Answer:—**Cha do dh'òl**, he didn't; or, **Dh'òl**, he did.

An do dh'fhan e aig baile ? Did he stay at home ?

Nach do dh'fhan e aig baile ? Did he not stay at home ?

Answer:—**Cha do dh'fhan**, he didn't; or, **Dh'fhan**, he did.

An do fhliuch e a chasan ? Did he wet his feet ?

Nach do fhliuch e a chasan ? Did he not wet his feet ?

Answer:—**Cha do fhliuch**, he didn't; or, **Fhliuch**, he did.

An do sgrìobh i an litir ? Did she write the letter ?

Nach do sgrìobh i an litir ? Did she not write the letter ?

Answer:—**Cha do sgriobh**, she did not; or, **Sgrìobh**, she did.

Sg, sp, sc, st, sm (except **sl**), **sn, sr** are not aspirated, for no one could pronounce them if they were.

In the above examples remember that **dh** is pronounced like "gh" in "ugh" unless the **dh** comes before **i** or **e** when it is pronounced as **y**.

Lesson No. 4a

Tha e cho fileanta ri bàrd. *He is as fluent as a rhymer.*

In English we try to make our words run as smoothly as possible, and so we do not pronounce each word separately. Try saying the phrase "Of course she does", and you will find yourself dropping the -se in "course" before "she". Or again, listen to a Canadian saying, "Where are you ?" What he really says is "wir a ye". The Gaelic speaker is no better in this respect than his neighbours.

Suppose when speaking of a person or thing, we use one of such little words as "at", "to", "from", "with", before the word "the", what happens is this: the **an** (or **am**) is shortened to **a'** and the first letter of the name word which follows is aspirated. Thus:—

an cat, the cat.	**air a' chat**, on the cat.
an gille (gēēl-y), the boy.	**leis a' ghille** (yēēl-y), with the boy.
am pàisde, the child.	**anns a' phàisde**, in the child.
am bùth (bōō), the shop.	**aig a' bhùth** (vōō), at the shop.

Now, consider these words:—**do**, to; **o**, from; **fo**, under; **de** (deh), of or from; **mu**, about. You will notice that they end in a vowel—remember our old friends of the school, **a, e, i, o, u**. After these instead of writing **a'** for "the" write **'n**. Thus:—

an cat, the cat.	**do'n chat**, to the cat.
am pàisde, the child.	**mu'n phàisde**, about the child.
an gille, the boy.	**o'n ghille**, from the boy.
am bùth, the shop.	**de'n bhùth**, of the shop.

24

With **pàisde** and **bùth** we would expect **mu'm phàisde** and **de'm bhùth**, but these are written and spoken with **de'n** and **mu'n** for no other reason than to be just like the rest. **An** meaning "the" coming before a name-word beginning with **d** and **t** will give you no trouble, for the **d** and the **t** are not aspirated. Thus we have:—

an teine, the fire.   **aig an teine**, at the fire.
an duine, the man.   **do'n duine**, to the man.

You will remember that we said in Lesson 3 that **f** when aspirated was silent. Take now the word **fàl** (fāh-l), a dyke. "On the dyke" would be **air an fhàl** (er un al), and so, too, in the case of the word **fear** meaning a man, "with the man" would be **leis an fhear**. We would not say **air a' fhàl** or **leis a'fhear** any more than you would say in English "a apple" or "a egg".

VOCABULARY

ann (ā-oon), in.
baile (bāl-y), town, homestead; **aig baile** (ek bāl-y), at home.
bòrd, a table.
cas (kass), a foot; **casan** (kāssn), feet.
casan (kāss-an), a footpath, a way.
ceart (kyā-rst), right, correct.
cheana (chēnna—ch as in loch), already.
cofi (kōf-fee), coffee.
còmhnard (kāw-nard), flat, level.
cruinn (krōōing), round.
dòirt ! (dāw-irst), pour ! pour out ! spill !
duilich (dōō-lich), sad, sorry.
fàg ! (fāh-k), leave!
fios (fēe-s), knowledge. Note.—**tha fios agam,** I know; **tha fhios agam,** I know it; **tha fios agad,** you know; **tha fios aige,** he knows; **cha n-eil fios agam,** I do not know; etc.

fosgail ! (fō-skal), open !

freagair ! (frāy-kir), answer !

gabh ! (gav), take ! accept !

gasda (gāss-ty), good, excellent.

geur (gāy-r), sharp.

gionach (gēē-nach), greedy.

glé (glay), enough, sufficient—aspirates the following word, e.g., **glé mhór**, big enough or quite big.

gloine (glōy-nye), a glass.

iomadh (ēē-ma), many.

ith ! (ee-ch), eat !

là, a day; **làithean** (lā-yin), days.

lasadain (lāssa-jin), matches.

leisg (laysh-k), lazy.

leugh ! (lay-v), read !

litir (lēē-tshir), a letter.

mìlsean (mēēl-shin), sweets, sweetmeats.

oir (or), for, because.

oisinn (ō-shain), a corner.

pàipeir (pȳ-pir—almost like the Cockney pronunciation of paper), paper.

pàisde (pash-tshy), a child.

pàirc (pahr-k), a park.

pòca (pāw-chk-y), a bag, wallet, pocket.

posta, postman.

ro (as in rose), very, too—aspirates the first letter of the following word, e.g., **ro-gheur**, very or too sharp.

saoghal (sāy-ul), world.

saoil ! (sāy-il), think !

saor-dhuais (sāir-ghōō-ash), pension.

seòladh (shāwl-uh), direction, address.

sguab ! (sgōō-up), brush ! sweep !

siùcar (shōōch-kur), sugar.

tì (tēē), tea.

trang, busy, throng.

trì (tree), three.

uair (ōō-ar), time, occasion; (pl.) uairean (ōō-ar-in), times, occasions. Note.—an uair a, when, e.g., an uair a bha e a' tighinn, when he was coming.

TRANSLATE INTO ENGLISH

An do chuir thu bainne anns a' chofi ? Cha do chuir oir shaoil mi gu'n robh bainne ann cheana. An do dh'ith iad na mìlsean a bha anns a' phòca ? Dh'ith. Bha iad gionach. Có bhris an copan sin agus có dhòirt an cofi air an ùrlar? An do dhòirt thusa (emphatic form of thu) e (it) ? Cha do dhòirt, ach tha mi ag creidsinn gu'n do dhòirt an duine so e. An do dh'fhàg am posta an litir aig an dorus an dé ? Cha do dh'fhàg, oir cha robh an seòladh ceart.

TRANSLATE INTO GAELIC

Did you put sugar in the tea ? I didn't. Did you take the matches that were on the table ? I didn't. Did she not sweep the path ? She didn't, for she was too busy. James has a nice dog. I know that, but did it not break its leg yesterday when it was running in the park ? It did, poor creature ! James is very sorry. Did you not read this book ? I did, and I am sorry, too.

SOLUTION OF LESSON 4

An do chuir thu siùcar anns an tì? Cha do chuir. An do ghabh thu na lasadain a bha air a' bhòrd? Cha do ghabh. Nach do sguab i an casan ?. Cha do sguab, oir bha i ro-thrang. Tha cù gasda aig Seumas. Tha fhios agam, ach nach do bhris e a' chas an dé an uair a bha e a' ruith anns a' phàirc ? Bhris, an creutair bochd ! Tha Seumas glé dhuilich. Nach do leugh thu an leabhar so ? Leugh, agus tha mi duilich cuideachd.

Lesson No. 5

*Is beò duine an déigh a shàrachaidh ach cha bheò e
idir an déigh a nàrachaidh. A man overwhelmed
still lives, a man disgraced does not.*

We saw in the first lesson how, if we wish to say "I have the
book", we put it in the form "the book is at me", i.e., **tha
an leabhar agam**. This, however, does not necessarily
mean that the book belongs to me. To say that the book is
mine and no one else's, we put it in the form, "the book is
with me", which is, translated, **is leam an leabhar** (iss
lāy-um un lyō-ur).

The word **is** is stronger than the word **tha**, and equals
the word "'tis" in English, so that **is leam an leabhar**
might be exactly translated by "'tis with me the book"; or,
in short, "the book is mine". Again, **Is leat** (leh-t) **an
leabhar** means "'tis with you the book", or "the book is
yours".

So, too, we can say, **is leinn** (lāing) **an leabhar**, i.e.,
"the book is ours". Also, **is leibh** (lāy-v) **an leabhar**, "'tis
with you the book," i.e., "the book is yours" (plural).

Notice in the above how

le joined with **mi** becomes **leam**.
le joined with **tu** becomes **leat**.
le joined with **sinn** becomes **leinn**.
le joined with **sibh** becomes **leibh**.

Curiously enough, however, **le** joined with **e**—him—
has become **leis** (lāy-sh), and **le** joined with **i**—her—has
become **leatha** (lēh-ha), and, lastly, **le** joined with **iad**—
they—has changed into **leo** (ly-o).

Notice, again, **is leam e** means "'tis with me it", i.e.,

28

"it is mine". **Is leat iad** means "'tis with you they", i.e., "they are yours"; and **is leis sin** means "'tis with him that", i.e., "that is his". **Is le Seumas, Màiri,** etc., so means "this is James's, Mary's, etc."

In past time we use **bu** instead of **is,** i.e., **bu leam an leabhar,** "'twas with me the book", i.e., "the book was mine"; **bu leis an sgian,** "'twas with him the knife", i.e., "the knife was his".

Now to continue.—We have feelings and desires as well as books and such like objects, and to express these feelings and desires we generally use **is** and **leam,** or if we are speaking of the past, **bu** with **leam, leat,** etc. For example, **toigh** (toy—pronounced very short) means agreeable or pleasant. **Is toigh leam** means "'tis pleasant with me", i.e., "I like"; e.g., **is toigh leam là blàth,** "I like a warm day"; **is toigh leis mìlsean, càise, airgiod,** etc., "he likes sweets, cheese, money, etc., and, in past time, **bu toigh leam an ceòl,** "I liked the music"; **bu toigh leo aran-milis** (mēēlish), "they liked pastry". Other useful phrases are:—**is duilich leam,** i.e., "'tis sad with me", i.e., "I am sorry"; **is feàrr** (fyār) **leam,** i.e., "'tis better with me," i.e., "I prefer". With regard to those phrases, compare the American slang "it's O.K. with me".

VOCABULARY

airgiod (ar-ri-kit), money.
anns a' mhaduinn (a-oons a vā-ting), in the morning.
aran-donn, brown bread.
aran-milis (ārran-mēēlish), pastry.
bean (ben), wife.
ceud nòt (kee-ut noh-t), a hundred pounds, i.e., £100.
coinneamh (kō-nye), meeting.
coisinn! (kō-shing), earn, win, gain.
có leis? (kō lāy-sh), whose ?
dad (dat), anything.

duais-sgrìob (dōō-ash skreep), sweepstake.
fèarr, (fyār), better.
monadh (mon-ugh), moor, moorland.

TRANSLATE INTO ENGLISH

(1) Is leam an sgian so, ach is leat an sgian sin.
(2) Có leis an sporan ? Am bheil airgiod agad ? Cha n-eil. Is duilich leam sin.
(3) Is le mo bhràthair an tigh sin air a' mhonadh.
(4) Is toigh leam cofi anns a' mhaduinn, ach is feàrr leat tì.
(5) Bu duilich leis nach robh airgiod aige.
(6) An do choisinn thu dad anns an duais-sgrìob ? Cha do choisinn, ach choisinn mo bhean ceud nòt.

TRANSLATE INTO GAELIC

The book is mine ('tis with me the book). The knife is James's ('tis with James the knife). There is a purse on the floor. It is mine ('tis with me it). You like brown bread, but he likes pastry. Were you at the meeting to-night ? I was not. I am sorry. The boat on the loch is mine.

SOLUTION OF LESSON 5

Is leam an leabhar. Is le Seumas an sgian. Tha sporan air an ùrlar. Is leam e. Is toigh leat aran-donn, ach is toigh leis aran-milis. An robh thu aig a' choinneamh an nochd ? Cha robh. Tha mi duilich. Is leam am bàta air an loch.

Lesson No. 6

Toiseach teachd agus deireadh falbh. *First to come, last to go.*

In English, when speaking of a young man, we may say,

(1) He is a youth,

or (2) He is in his youth.

To turn these into Gaelic we say:—

(1) **Is òganach** (āw-kan-ach) **e**, which means literally, "'tis a youth he (is)", i.e., "he is a youth".

or (2) **Tha e ann a òganach**, which means literally, "he is in his youth", i.e., "he is a youth", shortened into **tha e 'na òganach**.

Form (2) is the more common, but form (1) is used when we wish to leave no doubt as to what the person is.

Now, when we put **ann**, which means "in", in front of **mo, do,** etc., we get the following:—

ann+mo becomes **'nam.**
ann+do becomes **'nad.**
ann+a becomes **'na.**
ann+ar becomes **'nar.**
ann+bhur becomes **'nur.**
ann+an (or **am,** before **b, f, m, p**), becomes **'nan** (or **'nam**).

We saw in Lesson 3 that **mo,** my; **do,** thy; **a,** his, aspirated the words which followed, but **a,** her; **ar,** our; **bhur,** your; and **an** (or **am**), their, did not aspirate: this still holds good when they are joined with **ann**.

A few examples will make the use of these quite clear.

Is saighdear e, 'tis a soldier he (is); or, **tha e 'na shaigh-dear**, he is a soldier.

Is saor (sāȳ-ur) **mi**, 'tis a joiner I (am); or, **tha mi 'nam shaor**, I am a joiner.

Is cléireach (clāy-ruch) **thu**, 'tis a clerk you (are); or, **tha thu 'nad chléireach**, you are a clerk.

Is seudairean (shāy-dur-an) **sinn**, 'tis jewellers we (are); or, **tha sinn 'nar seudairean**, we are jewellers.

Is pìobairean (pēēp-ar-an) **sibh**, 'tis pipers you (are); or, **tha sibh 'nur pìobairean**, you are pipers.

Is fiaclairean (fēē-ach-klar-an) **iad**, 'tis dentists they (are); or, **tha iad 'nam fiaclairean**, they are dentists.

In the past time in Form (1) we use, instead of **is**, **bu**, which aspirates the following word unless it begins with a **d** or **t**. Thus:—

Bu phìobairean iad, i.e., they were pipers; and, **bu bhanarach i**, i.e., she was a dairy-maid; but, **bu dorsair** (dōr-sar) **e**, i.e., he was a door-keeper; and, **bu teine e**, i.e., it was a fire.

Just as in English we say, "he is in his youth", we say in Gaelic, "he is in his standing, running, sleeping", etc. Thus:

Tha mi 'nam sheasamh (hāyss-uv), literally, "I am in my standing", i.e., "I am standing; or in the past—

Bha mi 'nam sheasamh, literally, "I was in my standing", i.e., "I was standing" (compare the popular phrase, "I was on my mark".)

Tha (bha) thu 'nad shuidhe, ruith, chadal, etc., i.e., "you are (were) sitting, running, sleeping", etc.

Tha (bha) iad 'nan suidhe, ruith, cadal, etc., i.e., "they are (were) sitting, running, sleeping", etc.

VOCABULARY

armailt (ār-a-multsch), an army.
a' searmonachadh (shēr-mun-ach-ugh), preaching.

air an làr, on the ground.

bean-an-tighe (bēn-un-ta-ee), house-wife.

càirdean (kār-tshin), friends.

càr, tramcar, car.

chaidh (chā-eech), went.

chunnaic (chōō-nik), saw.

ciod e sin? (gu-dē-sheeng—pronounce sheeng as short as possible), what is that?

fada, long.

fear-an-tighe (fēr-un-ta-ee), house-man, the man of the house.

gu'n do chaill e, i (goon-dy-cha-eel eh, ee), that he, she, lost.

gu tinn, unwell, badly.

laidhe (lā-ee), lying, lying down.

làr, the ground.

mar sin, in that way.

mar so, in this way, thus.

ministear (mēēng-is-tshir), minister, clergyman.

stòl (stawl), stool.

tigh a' chofi, coffee-house.

TRANSLATE INTO ENGLISH

Ciod e sin? Is peann e. Tha iad 'nan iasgairean. Nach 'eil e fuar? Is fuar e. Bha e 'na rígh. Bu sheòla-dairean iad, agus bha sinne 'nar seòladairean cuideachd. (Sinne, stronger form than sinn). Is mi a tha duilich. Bha am ministear a' searmonachadh gu fada agus, mar sin, thuit an sluagh 'nan cadal. Chaidh mi leis a' chàr an dé agus chunnaic mi mo chàirdean 'nan suidhe ann an tigh a' chofi. Bha fear ag ràdh gu'n do chaill e airgiod a bha aige 'na phòca.

TRANSLATE INTO GAELIC

He is a young man. What is that at the door? It is a car. The dog was lying on the ground. My brother is a soldier. We were sitting on the stool. We saw James and Iain (ēē-an) when they were pipers in the Army. She was standing at the window. Were you (singular) asleep in the park to-day? I was. It was warm to-day, and I was tired.

SOLUTION OF LESSON 6

Tha e 'na òganach. Ciod e sin aig an dorus? Is càr e (or—**is e càr**). **Bha an cù 'na laidhe air an làr. Tha mo bràthair 'na shaighdear. Bha sinn 'nar suidhe air an stòl. Chunnaic sinn Seumas agus Iain an uair a bha iad 'nam pìobairean anns an armailt. Bha i 'na seasamh aig an uinneag. An robh thu 'nad chadal anns a' phàirc an diugh? Bha. Bha e blàth an diugh agus bha mi sgìth.**

Lesson No. 7

Cha n-eil i beag bòidheach no mór grànda. *She is neither tiny and pretty nor big and ugly.*

How often have we heard people say of a boat, or train "she is late to-night", or of a river in spate, "he'll be down on us soon"?

It is clear that we are not thinking that trains, boats and rivers have sex, just like men and women; indeed, it is only custom that makes us speak of the things around us as "he" or "she" as our forefathers did.

And, although this is not now so common as it was in English, apart from poetry, we find it quite usual in most other languages, and, of course, as we might expect, in an ancient tongue such as Gaelic.

As a result we shall have to get used to calling a table, a book, a house, a coat, etc., a "he" object, and a shoe, a chair, a river, a fine, etc., a "she" object; in a word, "he" objects are said to be masculine, and "she" objects feminine.

Now, those "she" or feminine words make certain changes in the sound of words beside them, e.g., **bòrd** (masculine) means "a table", and **bròg** (feminine), "a shoe". **Am bòrd** means "the table", and we might expect that **am bròg** would stand for "the shoe", but here the change takes place. The first letter of **bròg**, which is **b**, is aspirated, thus making **bh**, and the **am** becomes **a'**: hence we have **a' bhròg**, "the shoe".

Suppose, again, we say, "the big table". This is translated by **am bòrd mór**. But notice, however, "the big shoe" is rendered by **a' bhròg mhór**, the word **mór**, which tells us about the shoe, being aspirated, just like **bròg** itself. Further examples of this are:—

gille dubh, a black-haired boy.
caileag dhubh, a black-haired girl.

an gille dubh, the black-haired boy.
a' chaileag dhubh, the black-haired girl.

Again, **cù crùbach** means a lame dog; **bó chrùbach**, a lame cow; **an cù crùbach**, the lame dog; **a' bhó chrùbach**, the lame cow.

We saw in Lesson 4 that, to say anything in past time, we took the word of command and aspirated its first letter, thus:—

buail an cù ! strike the dog !
bhuail e an cù, he struck the dog.

This rule holds all throughout the language, except for some ten common words, which are easily remembered.

In English, for instance, we say "Go !" when we give an order, but, in the past time, "I went," using another form, as we can see. This sometimes happens in Gaelic, too, thus—**dean and rud so**, "do this thing", but **rinn** (rā-ing) **mi e**, "I did it". In the usual question and answer forms we have:—

An do rinn Seumas e ? i.e., did James do it ? **Nach do rinn Seumas e ?** i.e., did James not do it ? **Cha do rinn Seumas e**, i.e., James did not do it.

Now let us try another word. **Faic** (fā-eech-k) **sin !** see that ! And, in the past, **chunnaic mi e**, I saw it. In question and answer:—

Am faca (fāch-ka) **Seumas am bàta?** did James see the boat ? but **nach fhaca** (āch-ka) **Seumas am bàta ?** i.e., did James not see the boat ? and **cha n-fhaca Seumas am bàta**, i.e., James did not see the boat.

Note how, after **nach** and **cha**, we said, not **faca** but **fhaca**, which is easier to say; the **n** after **cha** is just to make the sound run smoothly.

VOCABULARY

an sin, there, then.
bàn (bāh-n), fair-haired, white.

balbh (bāl-uv), dumb.

beann (f) (byā-oon), hill.

beannaichte (byān-eech-tsheh), blessed, lucky, happy.

bodhar (bō-ar), deaf.

ceàrr (kyār), wrong.

clach (f) (klach—ch as in loch), a stone.

còmhradh (m) (kāw-ra), conversation, dialogue, chat.

crìoch (f) (krēē-uch), end.

dall (dāh-l), blind.

dàna (dāh-na), bold, cheeky, "gallus".

dona (dōn-a), bad.

droch (draw-ch), bad, evil.

e (eh), he, or a "he" object.

earraid (m) (ēr-ritch), policeman.

i (ee), she, or a "she" object.

idir (ēētsh-ir), at all.

làmh (f) (lāāv), hand; **làmhan** (lāvin), (plural), hands.

làthair (lā-hir), near, present.

leithid (lāy-hitsh), like; **a leithid**, his like, i.e., like him
    (Doric—The likes o' him).

o chionn ghoirid (ghāw-ritsh), a while ago.

rathad (rā-at) **mór** (m), road, highway.

riamh (rēē-uv), ever.

roimhe (rāw-ee), before.

sìos (shēē-us), down.

slaightear (m) (slȳ-tshir), rascal.

taobh (teh-v), side.

thar (har), over.

TRANSLATE INTO ENGLISH

(Masculine words). **Duine mór, an duine mór so.
Bàta beag, am bàta beag sin, mo bhàta beag. M'uan
beag. Ar tigh mór.**

(Feminine words). **Bean bhochd, a' bhean bhochd,**

a' bhean bhochd so. Beann àrd. A' bheann àrd sin
D' uinneag bheag. An litir fhada.

TRANSLATE INTO GAELIC

(Masculine words). The big house. The little stool.
A wet day. This warm fire.

(Feminine words). A big comb; this big comb. My
big sister. That little school.

SOLUTION OF LESSON 7

An tigh mór. An stòl beag. Là fliuch. An teine
blàth so.

Cìr mhór. A' chìr mhór so. Mo phiuthar mhór. An
sgoil bheag sin.

Note:—(1) **beann** is not used as often in speaking as
beinn (bey-ng) for a hill or mountain, unless one is speaking
of a number of hills or mountains, e.g., **cruachan beann**,
the cruachan or heap of hills or peaks. Have a look at it and
you will see how suitable the name is, and the Ben Mores are
usually big.

(2) **droch**, bad, is always put before the word to which
it refers, e.g., **droch dhuine**, a bad man, but **duine maith**,
a good man; and it always aspirates the word before which it
stands.

Lesson No. 8

Ged is dona an Donas thoir a chothrom dhà.
Although the Devil is bad give him fair play.

Suppose we wish to ask a question in future time, such as, "Shall I clean the window ?" we start, as we did in the case of past time, from the word of command, thus:—

Glan !—Clean !

An glan mi an uinneag ?—Shall I clean the window ?
Nach glan mi an uinneag ?—Shall I not clean the window ?
And the answer would be:—

Cha ghlan (mi an uinneag)—I shall not clean (the window),
or
Glanaidh (glān-eech) **(mi an uinneag)**—I shall clean (the window).
So, too,

Bris !—Break !

Am bris mi an uinneag ?—Shall I break the window ?
Nach bris mi an uinneag ?—Shall I not break the window ?

And the answer would be:—

Cha bhris (mi an uinneag)—I shall not break (the window),
or
Brisidh (brēēsh-eech) **(mi an uinneag)**—I shall break (the window).

As we see above, **-aidh** (or **-idh**) is added to the word of command to make a simple statement in future time, such as, I shall clean, break, run, dance, etc.: **-idh** alone is added when **i** is the last vowel in the word of command, as **bris, brisidh**: **cuir, cuiridh**.

Notice, too, that **cha** aspirates the first letter of the next word, unless that letter is a **t** or **d**—and, of course, it cannot aspirate a vowel. Thus:—

Cha tog mi a' chlach—I shall not lift the stone.
cha dùin (dōō-in) **mi an dorus**—I shall not shut the door.
cha n-fhan (n-an) **mi an so**—I shall not stay here.
cha n-òl mi e—I shall not drink it.

Cha takes **n** before a vowel for ease in speaking. **Fh** is, as we know silent.

Consider the following words:—Ox, brush, man, foot, mouse. If we wish to speak of more than one of these we say oxen, brushes, men, feet, mice. From these we see that there are two ways of forming what is called the plural. The first way is by adding a syllable to the word, thus:—ox, oxen; brush, brushes; and the second way is by making a change within the word itself, thus:—man, men; foot, feet; mouse, mice.

Now, in Gaelic, we find both ways of forming the plural, but the first way, which is more common, is by adding to the word **-an** (or **-ean**, if the last vowel of the word is an **i** or an **e**), e.g.:

bròg, a shoe; **bròg-an**, shoes.
làmh, a hand; **làmhan**, hands.
dorsair, a doorkeeper; **dorsairean**, doorkeepers.
sùil (sōō-il), an eye; **sùilean** (sōō-lin), eyes. (Compare the Scots **e'e**, an eye; and **e'en** , eyes).

The second way of forming the plural, as we saw, is by making a change within the word itself, e.g., man, men; foot, feet, etc. This change is caused in Gaelic (as it was in Old English) by an **i** being put after the last vowel of the word, e.g.:

balach, a boy; **balaich**, boys.
bàrd (bārst), a poet; **bàird**, poets.

But, just as in English, the **i** can make curious changes in the sound of the words, thus:—

mac (māch-k), a son; **mic** (mēēch-k), sons.

càrn (kārn), a heap or cairn; **cùirn** (kōō-irn), cairns or heaps.

ceann (kyā-oon), a head; **cinn** (keeng), heads.

fear (fer), a man; **fir** (feer), men.

each (ech), a horse; **eich** (ay-ch—ay as in "say"), horses.

beul (bel), a mouth; **beòil** (byāwl), mouths.

seòl (shawl), a sail; **siùil** (shōō-il), sails.

iasg, a fish; **éisg** (āysh-k), fishes.

The student should always use the **-an** (or **-ean**) plural in the exercises which follow, unless told otherwise. "The" in the plural is **na** or **na h-** before a vowel, thus, **na brògan, na mic, na fir, na h-eich, na h-éisg.**

VOCABULARY

brùid (brōōtsh), a brute, beast.

caidil! (kātsh-il), sleep!

cluinn! (klōō-ing), hear!

feumaidh (fāme-ee) **mi**, I must.

glasruich (glās-reech), vegetables.

Marbhphaisg (mār-ashk), a shroud, hence **marbhphaisg ort!** Curse you! lit., may a shroud be on you!

taingeil (taing-ul), grateful, thankful.

mi-thaingeil (mee-hāing-ul), ungrateful.

òran (āw-ran), a song.

salach (sā-lach), dirty.

sràid (srātsh), a street.

TRANSLATE INTO ENGLISH

Clach, a' chlach, clachan, na clachan.

Cas, mo chas, na casan, ar casan.

Sràid, sràidean, na sràidean so.

Eich, na h-eich, ar n-eich, bhur n-eich (n put after ar and
 bhur for ease in speaking), an eich.
Seòladair, seòladairean.
An cuir thu bainne anns an tì ?
Cha chuir, oir cha n-eil bainne agam.
Cluinnidh* tu na h-eòin a' seinn anns a' phàirc.
An tog iad na clachan sin ?
Togaidh, ach cha tog iad na clachan so.
Fàgaidh sinn am baile am màireach.
An caidil i an so an nochd ?
Cha chaidil, oir feumaidh i dol dachaidh.

*Cluinnidh tu may surprise you. Generally if the doing-
word ends in -dh, instead of writing thu, we write and say
tu, e.g., klōō-ing-ee too—where -ch drops out in speaking—
not kloo-ing-eech oo.

TRANSLATE INTO GAELIC

Hand; hands; the hands. Eye; the eyes; our eyes.
Boy; the boy; these boys. Son; my son; my sons; our
sons. Man; these men; the men. Your mouth. The
cairns. I will sing. We must go home. You will hear the
boys singing.

SOLUTION OF LESSON 8

Làmh ; làmhan ; na làmhan. Sùil ; na sùilean ;
ar sùilean. Balach ; am balach ; na balaich sin. Mac ;
mo mhac ; mo mhic ; ar mic. Fear ; na fir sin ; na fir.
Do bheul. Na cùirn. Seinnidh mi. Feumaidh sinn
dol dachaidh. Cluinnidh tu na balaich a' seinn.

Lesson No. 9

Ceann mór air duine glic is ceann circ' air amadan.
A big head on a wise man, a hen's head on a fool.

Take the following phrases:—

A boy's shoes, and
The boy's shoes.

Now these can also be written in another way, thus:—

(The) shoes of a boy, and
(The) shoes of the boy,

and this second form is the only way in which we can translate
them into Gaelic.

However, there is one little point to be noticed; the first
"The" (which we have put into brackets) is never translated,
so that when turned into Gaelic, "A boy's shoes" becomes
"shoes of a boy", i.e., **brògan balaich**, and "the boy's shoes"
becomes "shoes of the boy", i.e., **brògan a' bhalaich**. Now
we will explain how we get the words **balaich** and **a' bhalaich**.

Balach, as we know, means "a boy"; but "of a boy" is
balaich (bāl-eech), where an **i** has been put in after the last
vowel **a** of the word. Further examples are:—**crann** (krā-
oon), a mast; **crainn** (krā-ing—pronounced quickly), of a
mast. **Òran**, a song; **òrain** (āw-raing), of a song, etc. This
is the common way for masculine (or "he") words.

For feminine (or "she") words, we not only put in an **i**,
but also add a final **e**. Thus **bròg**, a shoe; **bròige** (brāw-
eek-eh), of a shoe. **Cluas** (klōō-as), an ear; **cluaise** (klōō-
ash-eh), of an ear. **Làmh,** a hand; **làimhe** (lāī-vy), of a hand.

In both masculine and feminine words, however, if the
last vowel is an **i**, **e** only is added, e.g., **féill** (fay-l) (fem.),
a fair or church festival, **là féille**, a fair or feast day. **Ìm**

(eem) (masc.), butter, and **cìr** (keer) (fem.), a comb, give **punnd ime**, a pound of butter and **fiaclan cìre**, teeth of a comb, not **iime** or **ciire**—the two **ii**'s are run together into one. **Tigh**, a house, **tighe**, of a house, does the same thing. **Ceisd** (kay-sht) (fem.), a question; **ceisde**, of a question.

Once more, **am balach** is "the boy", but "the shoes of the boy" is **brògan a' bhalaich**, where we notice the **b** of **balaich** has been aspirated and the **m** of **am** has been dropped for ease in speaking. So also we have **crann**, a mast; **crainn**, of a mast. **Bàrr crainn**, (the) top of a mast, or (a) top of a mast, but **bàrr a' chrainn**, (the) top of the mast.

Both "wets" and "drys" will find an easy way of remembering what letters aspirate after **a'** if they take the first letters of the words in the following phrase:—For Good Causes Many Prefer Beer.

An and not **a'** is written before **fh**, which, as we know already, is silent, e.g., **fraoch** (frāy-uch), heather. **Clann an Fhraoich** (klā-oon un rāy-eech), Children of the Heather. Remember never to aspirate the **d** or **t** of a word if an **n** comes before it, e.g., **deòch an doruis** (dyōch un dōrish), a stirrup cup (word for word, a, or the, drink of the door). **Ceann an tairbh** (tȳriv), the head of the bull.

Now let us try "of the . . ." before a feminine (or "she") word:—**bròg**, a shoe, but **na bròige**, of the shoe (not **a' bhròige**). **Sàil na bròige**, the heel of the shoe.

With feminine words "of the" in such phrases as "of the shoe, ear, hand, etc.", is always written **na** (or **na h-** before a vowel) and does not aspirate the first letter of the word which follows it, e.g., **craobh** (krāy-uv), a tree. **Bun na craoibhe** (boon—pronounced very shortly—na krāy-ev-eh), the foot of the tree. **Òraid** (āwr-itsh), a speech. **Crìoch na h-òraide** (krēē-uch na hāwr-itshy), the end of the speech.

VOCABULARY

a' rùdhrach (rōō-rach), searching.
bas (fem.), palm.

blas (masc.), taste.
cogadh (masc.) (kō-ka), war.
crioman (masc.) (krēē-mun), a piece.
cuspair (masc.) (kōō-spir), subject, material, theme.
dath (masc.) (da), colour.
féill (fem.) (fayl), a fair or church festival or feast.
feusag (fem.) (fēs-ak), whisker.
glas (fem.), lock.
mullach (masc.) (mōōl-ach), top.
na, that which, the thing which.
pòg (fem.) (pāw-k), a kiss.
slat (fem.), a rod.
sràid (fem.) (sratsh), a street.
taobh (masc.) (teh-v), side.
turus (masc.) (tōōrus), journey.

TRANSLATE INTO ENGLISH

Pòg, na pòige ; làmh, na làimhe, bas mo làimhe ;
slat, bàrr slaite, bàrr na slaite ; feusag a' chait ; leabhar
beag a' bhalaich ; crìoch a' chogaidh ; dath an
fhraoich ; glas an doruis ; aig taobh an rathaid ; aig
taobh na pàirce ; mullach an tighe ; air mullach
an tighe.

TRANSLATE INTO GAELIC

The taste of the butter. The end of the journey. The
head of the street. A piece of bread. The foot of the tree.
At the foot of the tree. The palm of the hand. On the palm
of the hand.

SOLUTION OF LESSON 9

Blas an ìme.   Crìoch an turuis.   Ceann na sràide.
Crioman arain.   Bun na craoibhe.   Aig bun na craoibhe
Bas na làimhe.   Air bas na làimhe.

Lesson No. 10

Cho glic ri sagart is eallach leabhraichean air. *As
wise as a priest with a load of books.*

A stranger in Glasgow would notice at once that the people
have many different ways of pronouncing the same word.
For instance, "hat" will be heard as "het", "hate", "hah-t",
or "ha'", thus showing that each district has its own way of
speaking. Of course, we all know what is meant when we
hear these different ways of saying the same English word.

Now, the reader who visits the Highlands may expect
something similar with Gaelic words, but there is this con-
solation—a great one, too—that the changes are not so many,
or so difficult. There is no standard pronunciation for Gaelic,
any more than there is for English.

If, now, the student will look back to Lesson 8, he will see
that we gave some examples of words which formed their plural by
putting an **i** after the last vowel of the word, instead of in the usual
way, by adding **an** (or **ean**), thus **balach**, a boy; **balaich**, boys.

In Lesson 9, we saw that **balaich** meant "of a boy";
thus, the same word **balaich** means "boys" or "of a boy".
Here are further examples of the same thing:—

bàrd, a poet; **bàird**, poets, or, of a poet.
òran, a song; **òrain**, songs, or, of a song.
cat, a cat; **cait**, cats, or, of a cat.

We saw in Lesson 8, however, that this **i** which we put
into the word can make curious changes in both sound and
spelling, e.g., **each**, a horse, becomes **eich**, which means
both "horses" and "of a horse". So, also we have:—

fear, a man; **fir**, of a man, or, plural, men.
càrn, a cairn; **cùirn**, of a cairn, or, plural, cairns.

ceann, a head; **cinn**, of a head, or, plural, heads.
mac, a son; **mic**, of a son, or, plural, sons.
beul, a mouth; **beòil**, of a mouth, or, plural, mouths.
iasg, a fish; **éisg**, of a fish, or, plural, fishes.
seòl, a sail; **siùil**, of a sail, or, plural, sails.

The same sort of changes are often found with feminine (or "she") words. Remember, however, to form the plural in the usual way by adding **an** (or **ean**). Thus:—

cas, a foot; **coise**, of a foot, but **casan**, feet.
cearc, a hen; **circe**, of a hen, but **cearcan**, hens.
long, a ship; **luinge**, of a ship, but **longan**, ships.
breug, a lie; **bréige**, of a lie, but **breugan**, lies.
clach, a stone; **cloiche**, of a stone, but **clachan**, stones.

There is an interesting point with regard to these feminine words which put in an **i** and add an **e**. For instance, a phrase such as "in the ship" is translated by **anns an luing**, which is just **luinge** without the final **e**. Further examples are:—

air mo bhròig, on my shoe, not **air mo bhròg**.
leis a' chloich, with the stone, not **leis a' chlach**.
aig a' chois, at his foot, not **aig a chas**.

Suppose, however, we want to say, "at the foot of the boy", "on the palm of my hand", "with the rod of the fisherman", or any such similar phrase, we write:—

aig cas (not **cois**) **a' bhalaich**.
air bas (not **bois**) **mo làimhe**.
le slat (not **slait**) **an iasgair**.

where the first name must always be written in its simple form, i.e., **cas**, **slat**, and **bas**, etc.

We have shown in Lesson 8 how to ask and answer questions in future time by using the word of command, thus:—

Bi deas (jace)! Be ready!

Am bi thu deas ? Will you be ready ?
To which the answer is:—

Cha bhi (vee) **mi deas**, I will not be ready, or simply **Cha bhi** ; or
Bithidh (bē-eech) **mi deas**, I will be ready, or simply **Bithidh**.

Cha, as we know, aspirates except when the following word begins with **t** or **d** (hence **bhi**).   In the plain statement **bithidh**, "I shall be ready", **th** (here silent) is put in merely to separate **bi** from **idh**, which has been added as in **brisidh**, **cuiridh**, etc. I shall break, put, etc.

VOCABULARY

a' falbh (fōl-uv), going away, going.
air bòrd (er bōrd), on board.
airgiod, money; **airgid**, of money.
an aghaidh (un ughy), against.
ath (a), next.
bratach (brāh-tach), banner, flag.
c'ar son ? (kar-sōn), why ?
cnoc (krōch-k), a hill (**cn** pronounced as **kr**).
dìrich (jēēr-eech), ascend, climb up.
eile (āīl-eh), another, other.
falt, hair.
gob (gope), a beak.
greim (graim), a hold, grip.
greusaiche (grēs-ich-eh), a shoemaker.
grian (grēē-un), the sun; **gréine** (graīn-ye), of the sun.
gu'm bi mi, thu, etc., that I shall be, you will be, etc.
leanabh (lyēn-uv), a child.
meud (māy-ut), amount, size, weight.
nach bi mi, thu, etc, that I shall not be, you will not be, etc.

neo-chadalachd (nyaw-chātal-achk), insomnia.
rothar (rāw-ur), a cycle.
rothaidhe (rāw-eech-eh), a cyclist.
rothaidheachd (rāw-ee-achk), cycling.
se (sheh), he, another form of **e**, he, used when followed by
    e, he; or, **i**, she.
solus, light.
ùr (oor), new.

TRANSLATE INTO ENGLISH

Mac ; mic ; do'n mhac ; na mic. Ceann an eich ;
air cas an eich. Sùil. Sùilean an éisg. Clach mhór ;
meud na cloiche ; le cloich ; leis a' chloich. Air bòrd
na luinge.

(1) Chuir an greusaiche sàil ùr air mo bhròig.

(2) Cha robh falt air ceann an fhir.

(3) Tha bean mo mhic ag ràdh gu'm bi i aig an tigh
am màireach.

(4) Am bi do bhràthair agus thu fhéin aig baile an
nochd ? Bithidh mise ach cha bhi mo bhràthair. C'ar
son ? Bha e a' rothaidheachd anns a' bhaile an dé,
agus bhuail e an aghaidh rothaidhe eile. Thuit mo
bhràthair agus an rothar air a chois agus bhris se i.

TRANSLATE INTO GAELIC

The flag of the ship. A bird; the beak of the bird; birds;
the birds. The sun; the light of the sun. The side of my
foot. At the foot of the horse. He struck the dog with a
stone. The boy's father found a purse on the road. We
climbed the hill and we put stones on top of the cairn. Will
the men be going away to-morrow ? They will not. Will
you be going? I will be.

SOLUTION OF LESSON 10

Bratach na luinge. Eun; gob an eòin; eòin; na h-eòin. A' ghrian; solus na gréine. Taobh mo choise. Aig cas an eich. Bhuail e an cù le cloich. Fhuair athair a' bhalaich sporan air an rathad. Dhìrich sinn an cnoc agus chuir sinn clachan air mullach a' chùirn. Am bi na fir a' falbh an màireach? Cha bhi. Am bi thusa a' falbh? Bithidh.

Lesson No. 11

Cha robh bàs fir gun ghràs fir. *No man died without a man being grateful.*

We have already seen that the usual way of saying "of a person" or "of a thing" was to put an **i** after the last vowel for masculine (or "he") words, and to add an **e** as well to the end of feminine (or "she") words.

Now language, like people, can be very contrary and sometimes the opposite of what I have just said takes place both in masculine and feminine words. For instance we put an **a** at the end of some words and further, if the word has an **i** as its last vowel, we knock its **i** out, e.g.:

bùth (bōō), a shop; **bùtha** (bōō-a), of a shop; **bùthan** (bōō-an), shops.

sùil, an eye; **sùla** (sōō-la), of an eye; **sùilean**, eyes.

But sometimes instead of **a** we find **ach** added, and, in the plural, **ach** (or **aich**) put in before adding **an** (or **ean**). For example:—

dàil (dāā-il), a meeting; **dàla** or **dàlach**, of a meeting; **dàlaichean** (dāl-eech-in), meetings.

machair (māch-ur), a plain; **macharach** or **machrach**, of a plain; **machraichean**, plains.

There are two things to be noticed here: (1) **macharach** is shortened to **machrach**, and (2) **dàlaichean** is written instead of **dàilaichean**.

Number 2 brings in a famous rule in Gaelic spelling, which says that if the last vowel of a syllable is an **i** or an **e** the first vowel of the next syllable must be either an **i** or an **e**; likewise if **a, o** or **u** be the last vowel of a syllable, the first vowel of the next syllable must be **a, o** or **u**, e.g., **bròg, brògan**, but **sùil, sùilean** and not **sùilan**. Hence in the example

51

above when we put **aich** between **dàil** and **ean** we had to drop the **i** of **dàil** and write **dàlaichean**.

A few other useful words are:—**athair**, a father; **athar**, of a father; **athraichean** (ār-eech-in), fathers. **Màthair**, a mother; **màthar**, of a mother; **màthraichean**, mothers. **Cathair** (kā-ir), a seat or city; **cathrach**, (kār-ach), of a seat or city; **cathraichean** (kār-eech-in), seats or cities. **Dùthaich** (dōō-eech), a country; **dùthcha** (dōō-cha), of a country; **dùthchannan** (dōō-chan-an), countries.

Many names of persons or things ending in a vowel (**a, e, i, o, u**) make no change except in the plural, e.g., **balla**, a wall, or, of a wall; **ballachan**, walls. **Coille** (kĭll-eh), a wood, or, of a wood; **coilltean** (kȳle-tshin), woods. **Fairge** (fār-rig-eh), a sea, or, of a sea; **fairgeachan** (fārg-eech-in), seas. **Oidhche** (ōō-eech-eh), night, or, of a night; **oidhchean** (ōō-eech-in), nights.

Now, suppose we want to use a phrase, such as "the boy was throwing a (or the) stone", we must write it in Gaelic as if it were "the boy was a' throwing of a (or the) stone", i.e., **bha am balach a' tilgeil** (tshēēl-ik-al) **cloiche** or **bha am balach a' tilgeil na cloiche**; also "climbing a (or the) tree" would be "a' climbing of a (or the) tree", and so on. Let us now try a plural form:—

Bha am balach a' togail chlach, i.e., The boy was (a') lifting (of) stones.

Bha am balach a' togail nan clach, i.e., The boy was (a') lifting (of) the stones.

Bha e ag càradh bhròg, i.e., He was (a') mending (of) shoes.

Bha e ag càradh nam bròg, i.e., He was (a') mending (of) the shoes.

Chlach, which is simply **clach** with the first letter aspirated, means "of stones"; likewise **bhròg** (i.e., **bròg** with the first letter aspirated), "of shoes". **Nan** (or **nam** before **b, f, m, p**) is used for "of the" before these "of" forms in the

plural, and takes away the aspiration. Hence **clach** and **bròg**
not **chlach** or **bhròg**.

VOCABULARY

a' bleàghadh (blēh-ugh); also **a' smocadh** (smochk-ugh),
    smoking, a pipe, etc.

ag càradh (kār-ugh), mending.

aighearach (ā-yer-ach), funny.

aig taobh (ek tēh-v), by the side of (followed by the "of"
    form of the next word).

air son, for the sake of, on account of (followed by the "of"
    form of the next word), Cf. Lesson 13.

am bliadhna (um-blēē-un-ah), this year.

am faod (fait), **mi, thu,** etc. May I, you, etc.

anabarrach (ān-a-bar-ach), tip-top, "ripping".

an uiridh (un-ōōr-ee), last year.

a' rannsachadh (rā-ōōn-sach-ugh), searching for.

a réir (a rāir), according to (followed by the "of" form of
    the next word). Cf. Lesson 13.

a' trusadh (trōōsh-ugh), gathering.

balachan, a little fellow.

barail, an opinion.

baralach, of an opinion.

beagan ùine (bake-an ōōn-ye), a little while.

caileag (kā-lak), a little girl.

caith (kye), spend, waste.

cladach (klāt-ach), shore.

cochlan (kāw-chlan), cigarette; plural, **cochlain.**

cròilean (krōy-lin), a club (of people).

fuaim (fōō-a-eem), a sound.

gann, scarce.

gàradh (gār-ugh), a garden.

guth (gōō), a voice; **gutha** (gōō-a), of a voice.

leabharlann (lyō-ar-lan), a library.

là saor (la sāir), a holiday; **làithean saora** (la-yin-sāira), holidays.

saighead (sȳ-itsh), an arrow; **saighde** (sȳ-jy), of an arrow.

sgeul (skāy-il), a story; **sgeil**, of a story.

ùirsgeul (ōōr-skil), a novel.

TRANSLATE INTO ENGLISH

Guth; fuaim a' ghutha; fuaim nan guth. Air son na cloinne. Aig ceann an locha. Air sràidean na cathrach. A' réir mo bharalach. Bha sinn aig taobh a' chladaich an uiridh, ach am bliadhna cha bhi làithean saora againn oir tha airgiod gann. Bha e 'na shuidhe anns a' chròilean ag òl cofi, a' bleaghadh chochlan agus ag innseadh sgéil aighearach.

TRANSLATE INTO GAELIC

The legs (feet) of the table; the legs of the tables. The size of that stone; the size of those stones. The top of the trees. We shall be leaving the town to-morrow. The little boy was standing at the shop window. I spent a little while in the library searching for (of) books, and I got a tip-top novel.

SOLUTION OF LESSON 11

Casan a' bhùird; casan nam bòrd. Meud na cloiche sin; meud nan clach sin. Mullach nan craobh. Bithidh sinn a' fàgail a' bhaile am màireach. Bha am balachan 'na sheasamh aig uinneag a' bhùtha. Chaith mi beagan ùine anns an leabharlann a' rannsachadh leabhraichean agus fhuair mi ùirsgeul anabarrach.

Lesson No. 12

"Mo chuid fhéin", "mo bhean fhéin" agus "théid sinn dhachaidh", na trì faclan as grinne anns a' Ghàidhlig. "My own goods", "my own wife" and "we will go home"—the three finest sayings in Gaelic.

In Lesson 5 we saw that when le (with) was put before **mi**, **tu**, etc., it joined up with these words and became **leam**, **leat**, etc.

Now, the same thing happens with the word **do**, which means **to**, when it is joined with **mi**, **tu**, **e**, **i**, etc.; only, some curious changes in sound and spelling have taken place, for which the reader must be prepared.

Do along with **mi** becomes **domh**, which means "to me"; **do** along with **tu** becomes **duit**, meaning "to you", and so on.

Now this would be fairly easy, only, in the course of time, Gaelic speakers have fallen into the habit of aspirating (i.e., putting an **h** after) the first letter **d** of all these words. As a result of this we have:—

dhomh (ghāw—gh as in ugh), to me.
dhuit (ghōō-tsch), to you.
dhà (ghā), to him.
dhi (or **dhith**) (ye), to her. (Cf. p. 18.)
dhuinn (ghōō-eeng), to us.
dhuibh (ghōō-eev), to you (plural).
dhaibh (ghā-eev, to them.

The simple forms are:—
domh (daw), to me.
duit (dōō-tsch), to you.

dà, to him.
di (jee), to her.
duinn (dōō-eeng), to us.
duibh (dōō-eev), to you (plural).
daibh (dā-eev), to them.

These simple forms are used after words which end in **d**, **n**, **t**. For example:—**thug e peann domh**, i.e., "he gave me a pen", but elsewhere the other forms are used. Examples:—**thug e dhomh mo thuarasdal**, i.e., "he gave me (or, more exactly, to me) my wages". **Innis dhuinn c'àite am bheil thu a' dol**, i.e., "Tell us (or, more exactly, to us) where you are going."

The reader will also remember how in Lesson 5 we used **leam**, with me, **leat**, with you, in phrases such as **is toigh leam**, i.e., "'tis pleasant with me", i.e., "I like"; and **is duilich leis**, "'tis sorry with him", i.e., "he is sorry".

Now, **domh**, **duit**, etc. (or **dhomh**, **dhuit**, etc.) can be used in much the same way. For instance:—**urrainn** (ōō-ring) means "possible". **Is urrainn domh**, "'tis possible to me", in short, "I can". **Is urrainn domh (duit, dà**, etc.) **snàmh**, "'tis possible to me (you, him, etc.) swimming", i.e., "I (you, he, etc.) can swim".

In past time, **bu** (or **b'** before **a, e, i, o, u**) takes the place of "is". Thus we would have **b'urrainn domh (duit**, etc.) **snàmh**, "'twas possible to me (you, him, etc.) swimming", i.e., "I (you, he, etc.) could swim".

Other words as well as **urrainn** can be used in this way. **Aithne** (āng-yeh) means "known" in such phrases as **is aithne dhomh**, "'tis known to me", i.e., "I know"; **is aithne dhomh gu'n robh e tinn**, i.e., "I know that he was sick"; **b'aithne dhomh gu'n robh e tinn**, "I knew that he was sick".

Once more:—**éiginn** (āīk-ing) means "necessary" in such phrases as, **is éiginn domh falbh**, "'tis necessary to me going", i.e., "I must go"; and in the past, **b'éiginn domh**

falbh leis an sguain (skōō-aing), "I had to go with the train". If my brother had to go with the train, we would say **b' éiginn do mo bhràthair falbh leis an sguain**, i.e., "my brother had to go with the train".

Now, if we wanted to put these phrases we have just learned in the form of questions (or answers), we would use the little words **an** (or **am**), **cha**, **nach**, whose acquaintance we have already made. Thus:—

An urrainn duit iomain ? "Can you play golf ?" **Nach urrainn duit iomain ?** to which the answer is either **is urrainn (domh iomain)**, "I can (play golf)", or **cha n-urrainn (domh iomain)**, "I can't (play golf)". Notice how **is** disappears in such phrases (and indeed always does so) after **an** (or **am**), **nach** or **cha**.

In past time, however, where we use **bu**, the **bu** is never dropped. For example, **am b' urrainn dà seinn ?** "could he sing ?" **nach b' urrainn dà seinn?** "could he not sing ?" to which the answer is either, **b'urrainn (dà seinn)**, "he could (sing)", or **cha b' urrainn (dà seinn)**, i.e., "he could not (sing)".

VOCABULARY

Alba (āl-a-pa), Scotland.
Albannach (āl-a-pannach), a Scot or Scottish.
an dìth-dhealg (jee-yāl-uk), the wireless, or **craolachan** (krēh-lachun), wireless.
a' soirbheachadh (sōr-riv-ach-ugh), prospering, doing well.
beart (byārst), a set.
beart dìth-dhealgach (yāl-uk-ach), a wireless set.
cè (kēh); also **uachdar** (oo-achk-ur) cream.
cè reòidhte (rāwtsh-eh), ice-cream.
cho dona sin, as bad (as) that.
chuala (chōō-ul-a, ch as in loch), heard.

cluich (klōō-eech), play; **dealbh-chluich** (jal-uv chlōō-eech), a stage-play.

deoch reòidhte, an iced drink.

dornadh (dōrn-ugh), boxing.

fanachd (fan-achk), staying, remaining.

faotainn (fāy-ting), getting. (**Ao** is more exactly pronounced as an Englishman would pronounce "ur" in such a word as burned.)

fo'n, under the.

gleachd (glēch-k), wrestling.

gleus (glāy-ss), tune, tune in.

gloine beòir (byāw-ur), a glass of beer.

iomain (ēēm-aing), golf, golfing.

is feàrr leam, I prefer.

ro-dhaor (ro-ghāīr), too dear. (Notice that **ro** aspirates.)

sabaid (sa-patch), a brawl, row, fight.

sgrùdadh-comais (skrōō-dugh-kō-mish), "Means Test".

teòm (tshōm), "dole"; **teòma**, of dole.

tuarasdal (tōō-ar-as-tal), wages, pay, salary.

TRANSLATE INTO ENGLISH

An urrainn duit rothaidheachd ? Cha n-urrainn, ach b' urrainn domh an uair a bha mi òg. B'éiginn duinn falbh leis a' bhàta. Am b'aithne do'n earraid am fear sin ? B' aithne gu maith.

Donald—An toigh leat cè reòidhte ?

Thomas—Is toigh, gu cinnteach, agus deochan reòidhte cuideachd, ach tha iad ro-dhaor an uair a tha duine bochd fo'n sgrùdadh-comais.

Donald—Tha sin fìor, ach cha n-eil mise cho dona sin, oir tha mi a' faotainn an teòma agus tha mo choch-lain agus gloine beòir agam air uairean.

Am bheil beart dìth-dhealgach agad ? Tha. Ghleus mi i an dé agus chuala mi cluich Albannach.

TRANSLATE INTO GAELIC

Can you play golf ? I can't now, but I could when I was young. Do you know my friend ? No, but I know his brother well. It was wet and we had to stay at home. Do you like boxing ? Yes, but I prefer wrestling.

SOLUTION OF LESSON 12

An urrainn duit iomain ? Cha n-urrainn domh a nis, ach b'urrainn domh an uair a bha mi òg. An aithne dhuit mo charaid ? Cha n-aithne, ach is aithne dhomh a bhràthair gu maith. Bha e fliuch agus b' éiginn duinn fanachd aig baile. An toigh leat dornadh ? Is toigh (leam), ach is feàrr leam gleachd.

Lesson No. 13

Talach a' ghille ghlic—'ga itheadh agus 'ga chàin-
eadh. *The shrewd youth's complaining—eating but
finding fault.*

Consider the sentence, **Fhuair e an t-airgiod ach cha do
rinn e an obair**, which means, "he got the money but he
didn't do the work". We notice that the word for "the"
before the word **airgiod** is written **an t-**, while before the
word **obair** it is written **an**. Not to worry the reader with
a long explanation, we may say that before a masculine (or
"he") word beginning with a vowel, "the" is written **an t-**,
but before a feminine (or "she") word there is no **t-**. For
example, **thog e an t-òrd agus bhris e an uinneag** means
"he lifted the hammer (masculine) and he broke the window
(feminine). Should, however, such little words as "to",
"from", "with", "by", "under", etc., come before the
masculine (or "he") word the **t-** is left out. For example,
"with the hammer" is in Gaelic, **leis an òrd**, not **leis an
t-òrd**: likewise, "on the floor" is **air an ùrlar**, not **air an
t-ùrlar**, and "at the place" is **aig an àite**, not **aig an t-àite**,
etc.

It is really a pity that the ladies should not have their **t**,
but the party is not over yet. If a feminine (or "she") word
begins with an **s** followed by a vowel or by one of the letters
l, n, or **r** (LiNeR), "the" is written **an t-**. Thus **sràid** means
"a street;" **an t-sràid** (un tratsh), "the street"; **air an t-
sràid**, "on the street"; **fo'n t-sràid**, "under the street";
so, too, **sròn** means "a nose"; **an t-sròn**, (un tràwn), the
nose (hence Troon); **air an t-sròin**, "on the nose". Notice,
however, **ceann na sràide**, "the head of the street"; **dath**
(da) **na sròine**, (sràwn-ye), "the colour of the nose," etc.,

60

where the **t** is not put in. Suppose, however, "of", "from", "with", "by", "to", or any such prepositions come before a masculine (or "he") word which begins with **s** followed by a vowel or by **l**, **n**, or **r** (LiNeR), then **an t-** is written instead of **an** to translate "the". Thus **saor** means "a joiner"; **an saor** (not **an t-saor**) means "the joiner"; but **mac an t-saoir** (un tāy-ur), "the son of the joiner" (hence the name Macintyre); **aig an t-saor**, "at the joiner"; **do'n t-saor** "to the joiner". In all those cases where the **t** is put in before **s** followed by a vowel or by **l**, **n**, or **r**, notice that the **s** is not pronounced.

Now let us try another matter. In English we say:—

"He did that on my account", which is in Gaelic:— **rinn e sin air mo shon** (hon). "On your account" would, of course, be **air do shon**; "on his account", or, if you like, "on account of him", **air a shon**; "on our account", or "on account of us", **air ar son**, etc. "On account of the boy" is **air son a' bhalaich**. From this last example we see that **air son**, which means "on account (of)" is always followed by the "of" form of the following word. There are many other simple but very handy phrases of the same kind which are used in the same way as **air son**. For instance, **am measg** (meesk) means "in midst (of)", i.e., among. "He came among us" will be **thàinig e an ar measg**, shortened to **thàinig e 'nar measg**.

Note.—**An** becomes **am** before **b**, **f**, **m**, and **p**, hence **am measg**, not **an measg**.

VOCABULARY

abhlan (āv-lan), a wafer.
an àite (un ātchy), in place (of), instead (of).
an d'fhuair ? (un dōō-ur), did (you he, etc.) get ?
an làthair (un lā-hir), in presence (of).

a réir (a rāir), according to —followed by "of" form of the next word.

beàrr ! (byārr), shave !

ceacht (kyecht), a lesson.

ceapaire (kēh-purra), a sandwich.

ciontach (kyōōn-tach), guilty.

clagan (klāg-an), a bell, a telephone bell.

coisiche (kōsh-eech-eh), a pedestrian.

Eadailteach (āy-dul-tschach), an Italian.

ealtuinn (yāl-ting), a razor.

e féin (eh fay-nn), also **e fhéin** (eh hay-nn and eh-hay) himself.

gluaistean (glōō-as-tshing), a motor car.

guthan (gōō-an), a telephone.

isbean (ēēsh-pang), a sausage.

leag ! (lake), knock down !

slaodan (slāy-tan), a cold.

sreath (sreh), a queue; **sreatha**, of a queue.

ugh (ōō), an egg; pl., **uighean** (ōō-een).

TRANSLATE INTO ENGLISH

An d'fhuair thu do bhrochan an diugh ? Fhuair agus isbeanan agus uighean cuideachd.

An do chuir an t-Eadailteach cè reòidhte air an abhlan ? Chuir agus rinn e ceapaire anabarrach dheth (of it).

Chuala an cléireach fuaim a' chlagain agus ruith e do'n (to the) ghuthan.

C'àite an d'fhuair thu an slaodan sin ? Fhuair mi e an uair a bha mi 'nam sheasamh aig ceann an t-sreatha an raoir.

TRANSLATE INTO GAELIC

In the eye; for the sake of his son; instead of the boy; in the presence of the king; among the trees. He shaved himself with the razor. According to my opinion, he was guilty. The motor knocked down the pedestrian in the street.

SOLUTION OF LESSON 13

Anns an t-sùil; air son a mhic; an àite a' bhalaich; an làthair an righ; am measg nan craobh. Bheàrr e e fhéin leis an ealtuinn. A réir mo bharalach (or mo bharail-sa) bha e ciontach. Leag an gluaistean an coisiche anns an t-sràid.

Lesson No. 14

Cha robh reithe leathann liath riamh reamhar.
*There has never been a broad gray fat ram. (A
tongue twister.)*

How often in our daily life do we hear such phrases as,
"trouble sits lightly on him", "he has a heavy cold on him"
—the idea being that troubles and colds, just like the "'flu",
are floating about in the air, ready to settle for good or ill
on somebody's shoulder.

In Gaelic we have the same idea. Joy, sorrow, hate,
shame, hunger, thirst, etc., are said to be "on" a person,
e.g.,

Tha an t-acras orm, which means "the hunger is on
me", i.e., "I am hungry".

Bha am pathadh (pā-ugh) **ort** (orst), which means "the
thirst was on you", i.e., "you were thirsty".

Orm, meaning "on me", comes from **air**, "on", joined
with **mi**; and **ort**, meaning "on you", comes from **air**
joined with **tu**. So, too, we have:—

Air joined with **sinn**, becoming **oirnn** (āw-ring), "on
us"; **air** joined with **sibh** becoming **oirbh** (āw-riv), "on
you" (plural); but

Air itself stands for "on him" as well as for "on"; **air**
joined with **i** becomes **oirre** (āw-ry), "on her"; **air** joined
with **iad** becomes **orra** (āw-ra), "on them".

We have already seen how phrases, such as "he was
standing, sitting, sleeping," were translated by **bha e 'na
sheasamh, 'na shuidhe, 'na chadal**, etc., which mean
really, "he was in his standing, sitting, sleeping", etc.

Now, bearing this odd way of speaking in mind, let us
consider a phrase such as, "he was striking me". We might

expect this to be turned into Gaelic by "he was a'striking of me", but, instead, we say, "he was at my striking", which is **bha e aig mo bhualadh**, shortened to, **bha e 'gam bhualadh**. "Striking you", would be **aig do bhualadh**, likewise shortened to **'gad bhualadh** ; "striking him", **'ga bhualadh**; "striking her", **'ga bualadh.**

A further example is, **thàinig e 'gar ('gur, 'gam) faicinn**, i.e., "he came to our (your, their) seeing", i.e., "he came to see us (you, them)". Remember that after **mo**, my, **do**, thy (or your), **a**, his, the following word is aspirated; but, after **a**, her; **ar**, our; **ur**, your; **an** (or **am**), their, there is no aspiration.

VOCABULARY

a chionn gu (a chy-ōōn-goo), because.
acras (āchk-ras), hunger appetite; **acrais**, of hunger.
a mach, out.
amadan (ām-at-an), a fool.
a nall (a-nāhl), over.
aroid (ā-rutsh), a table-cloth.
a' tòiseachadh (tāw-shach-ugh), beginning.
crùn (krōō-n), a crown, five-shilling piece.
dìol ! (jēē-ul), pay !
dìot bheag (jēē-utch-vake), breakfast.   Cf. French **petit dèjeuner.**
dìot mhór (jēē-utch vore), dinner.
dreuchdlann (drāy-uchk-lan), an office.
gu h-olc, badly.
gu'n robh maith agad ! (gōō-ro-mā-akut), thank you !
lach, bill, account.
mas e do thoil e (mash-eh-do-hōl-eh), if you please.
meas-cheapairean (māyss), fruit sandwiches.
modhail (māw-ul), polite.
mùthadh (mōō-ugh), change (money).
nàire (nāh-ry), shame.

ruisean (rōōsh-in), lunch.
ruisein, of a lunch.
sìn! (sheen), hand over! Notice that **sin** means "that".
sraidheag (srā-ug), cake.
thoir dhomh! (hāwr-ghaw), give (to) me!

TRANSLATE INTO ENGLISH

Am bheil an t-acras ort? Cha n-eil ach tha am pathadh orm. An gabh thu copan tì? Gabhaidh, gu'n robh maith agad!

Bha fearg mhór oirre a chionn gu'n do dhòirt fear an tighe an tì air an aroid.

Thoir dhomh an cofi mas e do thoil e. Sìn a nall dhomh na meas-cheapairean.

Am bheil mùthadh crùin agad? Cha n-eil, oir dhìol mi an lach.

C'àite am bheil thu a' dol air son do ruisein? Cha n-eil mi a' dol a mach an diugh idir. Gabhaidh mi sraidheag agus copan tì anns an dreuchdlann.

Is toigh leam an t-òran sin, ach tha an t-amadan 'ga sheinn gu h-olc.

Thàinig e dachaidh agus ghabh e a dhìot mhór.

TRANSLATE INTO GAELIC

He was ashamed; they were angry; we were hungry; my friend was thirsty. Hand over that book if you please. That boy is polite for he said "Thank you" when I gave him the prize. He was telling me that his brother was deaf and dumb.

SOLUTION OF LESSON 14

Bha nàire air; bha fearg orra; bha an t-acras oirnn; bha am pathadh air mo charaid. Thoir dhomh (or

sìn dhomh) an leabhar sin, mas e do thoil e. Tha am
balach sin modhail, oir thubhairt e "gu'n robh maith
agad" an uair a thug mise dha an duais. Bha e ag
innseadh dhomh gu'n robh a bhràthair bodhar agus
balbh.

Lesson No. 15

Trì nithean a thig gun iarraidh—gaol, eud agus
eagal. *Three things that come unasked—love, envy
and fear.*

The numbers in Gaelic run pretty much the same as in
English. Here they are up to ten:—

aon (oon), one.	**sè** (sheh), six.
dà, two.	**seachd** (shech-k), seven.
trì (tree), three.	**ochd** (och-k), eight.
ceithir (kāy-ur), four.	**naoi** (nōō-ee), nine.
còig (kō-ik), five.	**deich** (jay-ch), ten.

A little point worth noticing is that **dà** aspirates the first
letter of the following word, unless that word begins with a
vowel, which, of course, cannot be aspirated.

The word which means "one", viz., **aon**, is like **dà**, for it
aspirates the first letter of the following word unless that word
begins with a vowel; but more, it does not aspirate words
beginning with **d, t, s**, so, to help you to remember, DaTeS.

Examples:—**aon each, long, mhionaid, tigh, uair,**
etc., i.e., "one horse, ship, minute, house, hour", etc. **Còig
eich, seachd longan, naoi mionaidean, deich uairean,**
i.e., "five horses, seven ships, nine minutes, ten hours".

The 'teens in Gaelic start at eleven instead of at thirteen
as in English, and the word for "teen" is **deug** (jāy-k). Thus
aon deug means "eleven"; **dà dheug,** "twelve"; **trì deug,**
"thirteen"; and so on to **naoi deug,** "nineteen"; and
fichead (fēēch-ut), "twenty".

The reader will remember how the old proverb says:—

Twa men an' ten withouten skaith.
Sit three an' ten—the'll be a daith.

68

Now this old way of counting is still employed in Gaelic. Thus **trì brògan deug** means "three shoes (and) ten", i.e., "thirteen shoes"; **ochd mionaidean deug** means "eight minutes (and) ten", i.e., "eighteen minutes"; **còig mionaidean fichead**, means "five minutes (and) twenty", i.e., "twenty-five minutes".

Now to turn to another walk of life. We are again using another old-fashioned way of speaking in English when we say, "two stone", "twenty ton", "a hundred ton", and so on, instead of "two stones", "twenty tons", or "a hundred tons", and this is just what we say in Gaelic, too. For instance, **dà rìgh** (not **dà rìghean**) means "two kings"; **fichead fear** (not **fichead fir**), "twenty men", and **ceud punnd**, "a hundred pound(s)".

Notice that it is only with the words for "two", "twenty", "a hundred" and "a thousand" that this occurs.

VOCABULARY

an ceart uair (un gyārstar), the exact hour, i.e., just now.

an dèidh (un-jāy-gh), after.

air dheireadh (air-yāīr-ugh), late, behind.

air maduinn (air māt-ing) **an diugh**, in the morning, to-day, i.e., this morning.

a steach (ah-stech), in.

bonn-a-sè (bōne-a-sheh), a halfpenny.

caolbhain (kēēl-ah-veen), lead pencil; Scots "keelyvine".

coltach (kōl-tach), like.

cia mar a (kēh-mar-a), how or what way.

Is e do bheatha (ishēh-do-veh-a), you are welcome. This is a phrase of great interest, for it really means, "it is your life".

mar sin leatsa, same with you; Cf. the slang, "same to you".

mìle (mēēl-uh), a mile.

mu (moo), about.

sgillinn (skēēl-ing), penny (scots money).

slàn leat, good-bye, "ta-ta".
suathan (sōō-a-han), rubber.
thig ! (hēēk), come !

TRANSLATE INTO ENGLISH

Naoi fir. Sè leabhraichean. Ceithir longan fichead.
Fichead nòt. Ceud mile. Bha an sguain cóig mionaidean air dheireadh air maduinn an diugh. Tha seachd
sgillinn agus bonn-a-sé agam 'nam phòca. Thig a
steach ; is e do bheatha. Thàinig e 'na ghluaistean an dé
mu aon uair deug, agus tha e 'na dhreuchdlann an
ceart uair. Cia mar a tha thu ? Tha gu maith. C'àite
am bheil thu a' dol ? Tha mi a' dol dachaidh. Slàn
leat. Agus mar sin leatsa.

TRANSLATE INTO GAELIC

Three men; five boys; fifteen minutes; eleven hours.
He lost his pencil and his rubber. He went twenty miles on
his bicycle. I left the office at 12.25 and went for a coffee to
the club, and when I had my lunch I came back to my office
at 1.45.

SOLUTION OF LESSON 15

Trì fir ; cóig balaich ; cóig mionaidean deug ; aon
uair deug. Chaill e a chaolbhain agus a shuathan.
Chaidh e fichead mìle air a rothair. Dh'fhàg mi an
dreuchdlann aig cóig mionaidean fichead an déidh dà
uair dheug, agus chaidh mi air son cofi do'n chròilean
agus an uair a fhuair mi mo ruisean, thill mi do mo
(do m'—short form) dhreuchdlann aig cóig mionaidean
deug do dhà uair.

Lesson No. 16

Na'm b'e an diugh an dé! *Were to-day yesterday!*

In the last Lesson we gave a question "on the clock". Perhaps the reader thought it hard to answer, but really it is quite easy, for we tell the time in Gaelic in much the same way as we do in English.

Certain words you must remember are:—**o**, from; **do**, to; **mu**, about;—all of which aspirate—and **an déidh** (un-jāy-gh), after.

Thus the man who left his office at 12.25 (for a coffee) would say, **dh'fhàg mi an dreuchdlann aig cóig mionaidean fichead an déidh dà uair dheug** (yāke), i.e., "five minutes (and) twenty after two hours (and) ten".

And as he came back at 1.45, he would say, as in English, **thill mi aig cairsteal do dhà uair**, i.e., "I returned at a quarter to two".

Cairsteal (kārst-yal) means "a quarter" and is more used than **cóig mionaidean deug** for "fifteen minutes".

Further examples are:—**thàinig e aig aon uair deug**, i.e., "he came at eleven o'clock"; **dh-éirich a' ghrian aig cairsteal an déidh cóig** (**uairean**—understood), i.e., "the sun rose at a quarter past five"; **tha e mu sheachd uairean**, i.e., "it is about seven o'clock". Note that **uairean** may often be left out.

Nowadays when counting in Gaelic we usually put an **a** in front of the number, **a h-** before a vowel for ease in speaking.

Thus:—**a h-aon**, one; **a trì**, three; **a ceithir**, four; **a h-ochd**, eight; **a h-aon deug**, eleven; **a fichead**, twenty. Curiously enough instead of saying **a dà** we say **a dhà** (a ghā) for two.

The use of **a** before numbers need not cause you any

trouble, for this **a** is used only when the name of the person or thing is not mentioned along with the number.

Thus in answer to the question, "how many men are here ?" you can say either, **a trì**, or **trì fir**, but not **a trì fir.**

Having settled the hour of the day, we will now go on to the days themselves. They all begin with **di** (jee), an old word which means "a day".

Monday is **di-luain** (jee lōō-aing), the day of the moon; Tuesday is **Di-màirt** (jee-màrst), the day of Mars. The next three days are very interesting for their names refer to the fast days of the early church. **Di-ciadaoin** (jee-kēē-a-ting) is the day of the first fast which fell on Wednesday; **Di-ardaoin** (jeer-dāy-ing) is the day between the first fast and **Di-h-aoine** (jee-hāīn-yeh), Friday, the day of the (great) fast. Saturday is **Di-sathuirn** (jee-sā-hurn), or the day of Saturn, while Sunday is **Di-dòmhnuich** (jee-dāwn-ich), the Lord's Day. Examples:—

Bha sinn aig a' phreaban air Di-sathuirn, "we were at the circus on Saturday"; **thàinig e air feasgar Di-h-aoine**, "he came on Friday evening", **agus dh'fhalbh** (ghōl-uv) **e air maduinn Di-luain**, "and he went away on Monday morning".

VOCABULARY

a' feitheamh (a-fāy-uv), waiting.

a réir coltais (a rair kōl-taish), in all likelihood, apparently.

Ceilteach (kāil-tshach), Celtic.

chaidh, past (or, went).

crìochnaich ! (krēē-uch-neech), finish !

cloichead (klōych-it), passport.

c'uin ? (kōō-ing—pronounced very quickly), when ?

deantach (jānt-ach), an agent.

deireadh (jāy-rugh), end, conclusion.

Eadailt (āy-daltsh), Italy. **An Eadailt**, The Italy (see France).

faiche (fȳ-eech-eh), a playing field, sports ground.

Faiche nan Ceilteach, Celtic Park, a famous sports ground in Glasgow.

Fraing (frā-ing), France. **An Fhraing** (un rā-ing), i.e., The France, just as The Netherlands in English.

Gearmailt (gērmult), Germany. **A' Ghearmailt** (a yēr-mult), The Germany.

geartach (gēr-tach), excursion.

giustal (gyōō-stal), sports.

leth (l-yāy), a half; **leth-uair**, half hour, or, "half", in time.

mìos (mēē-us), a month; **mìosa**, of a month.

oda, a race-course. (Up till about a century ago, race-meetings were very popular in the Highlands.)

preaban (prāy-pan), a circus.

rib (reep), a hair.

ris (reesh), for or to.

searrag (shār-uk), a bottle.

sgàil-bhothan (skal-vāw-an), a shelter.

snodhach (snāw-ach), hair-restorer.

Spàinnt (spā-int), Spain. **An Spàinnt**, The Spain (see France).

till! (tshēēl), return!

tòisich! (tāwsh-eech), begin!

TRANSLATE INTO ENGLISH

Ciod e an uair a tha e? Trì uairean. Tha sinn a' dol do'n Fhraing air geartach aig deireadh a' mhìosa so. Bha mi 'nam sheasamh fichead mionaid air oidhche Di-luain anns a' sgàil-bhothan a' feitheamh ris a' chàrr. Bha sinn aig a' ghiustal air Di-sathuirn so chaidh ann am Faiche nan Ceilteach. Cheannaich an duine bochd searrag snodhaich air feasgar Di-luain, agus air maduinn Di-ciadaoin cha robh rib 'na cheann idir. Bha ar deantach anns an Eadailt a' mhìos so chaidh, tha e anns a' Ghearmailt a nis, agus a réir coltais bidh (or **bithidh**) e anns an Spàinnt air a' mhìos so tighinn.

TRANSLATE INTO GAELIC

2.15; 3.20; 5.30; 7.45; 9.10; 12.15.

I was at the race-course on Tuesday. When did your agent get his passport ? On Monday morning. The meeting started at seven o'clock on Thursday evening and finished at twenty-five minutes to twelve. The excursion went away on Thursday morning at 9.30 and returned in the evening about 7.45.

SOLUTION OF LESSON 16

Cairsteal an déidh dà uair ; fichead mionaidean an déidh trì ; leth-uair an déidh còig ; cairsteal roimh ochd ; deich mionaidean an déidh naoi ; cairsteal an déidh dà uair dheug. Bha mi aig an oda air Di-màirt. C'uin a fhuair do dheantach a chloichead ? Air maduinn Di-luain. Thòisich a' choinneamh aig seachd uairean air feasgar Diardaoin agus chrìochnaich i aig cóig mionaidean fichead roimh dà uair dheug. Dh'fhalbh a' gheartach aig leth uair an déidh naoi air maduinn Diardaoin agus thill i anns an fheasgar mu chairsteal roimh ochd.

Lesson No. 17

Cha bhòrd bòrd gun aran ach is bòrd aran e fhéin.
*A table is no table without bread but bread is a table
itself.*

This lesson will be, like Dickens' "Old Curiosity Shop", a
"gether-up o' uncos an' auld nick-nackets", but it won't be
any the less interesting on that account, we hope.

Who would suspect the little word **in** of being troublesome?
And yet it is so, even to Gaelic speakers and writers themselves.

Only the other day we heard one man, in answer to the
question, "Whaur did ye get that?" say, "Och! A got it in
in a book."

Now, although that man did not know it, he was saying
just what is said in Gaelic, **Och! Fhuair mi e ann an
leabhar.**

Note, then, that when **in** comes before **a** it is written **ann
an**, but before **the** it is written **anns**.   Examples:—

ann an ùirsgeul, in a novel; but **anns an ùirsgeul**, in the
novel.

ann am preaban, in a circus; but, **anns a' phreaban**, in
the circus.

ann an cròilean, in a club; but, **anns a' chròilean**, in
the club.

ann am faiche, in a sports ground; but, **ann am Faiche
nan Ceilteach**, in the Celtic Park, i.e., in the park of
the Celts.

In the last example remember that the first "the" is not
translated.   (See Lesson 9).

Do meaning "to", is also a tricky little word. If it is followed by a vowel (**a, e, i, o, u**) or by an **f** with a vowel after it, it is also doubled. Take the phrase, "he is John's son". This would be turned into Gaelic in the form "'tis a son to John he (is)", i.e., **is mac do dh'Iain e.**

Notice how **do** has been doubled, the second **do** being written **dh'**. This **do dh'** is usually watered down to **a dh'**, as you may remember from Lesson 4.

Something the same happens in English. For instance, "he is going to sing" has got worn down to "he is gonna sing", where "to" has become "a" at the end of "gonna".

Examples:—

"He is going to Ireland", **tha e a' dol a dh'Eirinn.**
"He went to fish", **chaidh e a dh'iasgach.**
"He is going to stay", **tha e a' dol a dh'fhanachd.**

Here we may say that **do** in all its forms (**do, dh', a**) aspirates.

"He is going to sleep", **tha e a' dol a chadal.**
"He is going to sing", **tha e a' dol a sheinn.**
"He is going to answer", **tha e a' dol a fhreagairt.**
"He is going to answer the question", **tha e a' dol a fhreagairt na ceisde.**

The reader will remember how we said in Lesson 11 that a sentence like "he is striking the door" was turned into Gaelic in the form, "he is a' striking of the door", i.e., **tha e a' bualadh an doruis.**

In the same way, "he is going to answer the question" is put into Gaelic in the form, "he is going to (the) answering of the question", as above.

VOCABULARY

Abair-Eadhain (apir-ēh-un), Aberdeen.
buntata (poon-tā-ta), potato.

caladh (kāh-la), harbour.

dùnadh (dōōn-ugh), closing.

Dùn-Éideann (doon-āītsh-in), Edinburgh.

dùsgadh (dōōsk-ugh), wakening.

glan! clean!

glasruich (glās-reech), vegetables.

luag (lōō-ak), a doll.

luidhear (lōō-yir), chimney.

sguabair (skōō-up-ir), sweep, sweeper.

sùgh donn (sōō-don), brown soup.

thachair air (hāch-ur), come upon, happen to meet.

tigh-eiridinn (āīr-itsh-in), hospital, nursing-home.

toiteach (tāwtsh-ach), steamer.

toitean (tāwtsh-in), chop.

TRANSLATE INTO ENGLISH

Thàinig an t-earraid a dhùsgadh mo bhràthar aig sé uairean. Dh'fhalbh e a dh'fhaicinn nan toiteach anns a' chaladh. Dh'éirich i a dhùnadh na h-uinneig. Thachair mo bhràthair air Iain anns an tigh-eiridinn. Am bheil tu a' dol a dh'Eirinn? Cha n-eil, oir cha n-eil an t-airgiod agam. Ciod e a bha agad mar ruisean an diugh? Bha sùgh donn, toitean, buntata agus glasruich.

TRANSLATE INTO GAELIC

He went to Edinburgh by the train. The book is in a library at Aberdeen. The girl went into the shop to buy a doll. We shall see you on Tuesday evening at 7.30. The sweep came to clean the chimney.

SOLUTION OF LESSON 17

Chaidh e do Dhùn-Éideann anns a' sguain. Tha an leabhar ann an leabharlann ann an Abair-Eadhain. Dh'fhalbh a' chaileag bheag a steach do'n bhùth a cheannach luaig. Chì sinn thu aig leth-uair an déidh seachd feasgar Di-màirt. Thàinig an sguabair a ghlanadh an luidheir.

Lesson No. 18

Na sir 's na seachain an cath. *Neither seek nor shun the fight.*

Up till now we have been dealing with hard facts, but in this lesson we are going to speak about things that might happen. For example, we might say, "I would bet a shilling on that, if I had the money": and to turn sentences of this kind into Gaelic is quite easy.

If we want to say that a person should or would do anything, we take the doing word in past time and tack **-adh** on at the end, or **-eadh** if the last vowel is an **i** or an **e**. Thus :—

thog e, he lifted; **thogadh** (hōk-ugh) **e**, he would lift.

bhris sibh, you broke; **bhriseadh** (vrēēsh-ugh) **sibh**, you would break.

But notice:—

thogainn (hōk-ing), I should lift; **thogamaid** (hōk-a-mitsh), we should lift.

bhrisinn, I should break; **bhriseamaid**, we should break.

Here **-ainn** (or **-inn** after **e** or **i**) stands for "I should", and **-amaid** (or **-eamaid** after **e** or **i**) for "we should".

The reader will remember that in Lesson 4 we learned how to use the little words **an, an do, cha** and **nach**; e.g., **an òl e**, will he drink; **nach bris e**, will he not break, and so on. Other little words just as important are:—**mur** which means "unless", "if not"; **ma**, which means "if", and **ged** which means "although". This is how they are used:—

ma thuig e sud, if he understood that, and
ma dh' òl e beòir, if he drank beer.

79

ged a thuig e sud, although he understood that, and
ged a dh' òl e sud, although he drank that.

mur an do thuig e sud, unless he understood that, and
mur an do dh' òl e sud, unless he drank that, if he did not
drink that.

Notice that **ma** always aspirates, that **ged** is followed by
a and that **mur** takes **an do** after it in the past. Now in the
present we have:—

mur tuig e so, unless he understands this, and
mur òl e sin, unless he drinks that.
mur pàidh (pȳ-ee) **e a mhàl**, unless he pays his rent.
ma thuigeas e so, if he understands this.
ma dh' òlas e so, if he drinks this, and
ma phàidheas (fȳ-yus) **e a mhàl**, if he pays his rent.
ged a thuigeas e so, although he understands this, and
ged a dh' òlas e so, although he drinks this.

The ending **-as** (and **-eas**) is always found at the end of the
doing word in the present when **ma** or **ged a** comes before
it. You will remember from Lesson 8 to use **-as** if the last
vowel of the doing word is **a**, **o**, or **u**, but **-eas** if the last
vowel is either **e** or **i**.

These endings crop up again where one would least expect
them. Consider the English:—"the man who struck the
dog". This turns into Gaelic word for word, **an duine a
bhuail an cù**; but if we ask the question:—"who struck the
dog ?" we must say, **cò a bhuail an cù ?** You should notice
that **có a** is usually reduced to **có** so that we have **có bhuail
an cù** or **có dh' òl am beòir ?** If we want to find out who
drinks the beer, we ask **có a dh' òlas am beòir**, and as we
have just said **có a** is cut down, so that we have **có dh' òlas
am beòir ?** On the other hand, if we know who drinks the
beer and we are going to speak about him, we say **an duine
a dh' òlas am beòir**, the man who drinks the beer, **an duine
a dh' itheas sin**, "the man who eats that, "and **an duine a**

bhuaileas an cù, "the man who strikes the dog". Notice
that in these last examples, however, the a must not be left
out: the a is left out only after có meaning who ?

Now to return. More often than not we "hae oor doots"
about our wishes coming true, and Gaelic is equal to the
occasion. Thus:—na'n tairgeadh (tār-rig-ugh) e tabhartas
(tav-ar-tus), ghabhainn (ghā-ing) e, i.e., "if he would offer
a tip, I should take it".

Of course, I don't expect that he will offer it, and so I
use na'n instead of ma.

So, too, mur pàidheadh e an t-airgiod, bhitheadh e
amaideach (ā-mitsh-uch), i.e., "if he would not pay the
money, he would be foolish".

When na'n and mur are used with "should" or "would"
forms of a word, we drop the aspiration and hence tairgeadh
and pàidheadh, and not thairgeadh and phàidheadh.

VOCABULARY

bith! (be), be!
cluich (klōō-eech), game.
geall! (gyā-ool), promise!
reic! (rāy-ichk), sell!
stad! (stat), stay!
sgìth (sgee), tired.
teich! (tshāy-ch), flee!
thubhairt (hōō-irtsh), said.
toilichte (tāw-leech-tshe), pleased.
tubaist (tōōp-isht), accident.

TRANSLATE INTO ENGLISH

Bhrisinn; bhriseamaid; thogadh iad; thogainn;
bhriseadh e. Thilgeadh iad; stadadh sibh; thilginn na
clachan; dhòirtinn an ti. Ma thubhairt e sin, bha e

ceàrr. Na'n tigeadh e dachaigh, bhitheamaid toilichte.
Mur an do thog Dòmhnull an t-airgiod, có thog e ?
Ma chunnaic e an tubaist, c'arson nach do dh'innis e
sin do'n earraid ?

TRANSLATE INTO GAELIC

I should read; we should lift; you would lift; he would
flee. I should stop; they would promise; they would sell;
you would strike. If you didn't break the window, who did ?
If you have the money, will you pay me ?

SOLUTION OF LESSON 18

Leughainn ; thogamaid ; thogadh tu ; theicheadh
e. Stadainn ; ghealladh iad ; reiceadh iad ; bhuaileadh
tu. Mur an do bhris thusa an uinneag có a bhris i ?
Ma tha an t-argiod agad am pàigh thu mi ?

Lesson No. 19

Ged bu dona an saor bu mhaith a shliseag—mar a
thubhairt a bhean an uair a chaochail e. *Although
the carpenter was bad yet his shavings were good—as
his wife said when he died.*

In Lesson 14 we showed how to turn into Gaelic a phrase
like, "he is striking me". We put it in the form:—"he is at
my striking", i.e., **tha e aig mo bhualadh**, or **tha e 'gam
bhualadh**—'gam being the short way of saying **aig mo**,
"at my". So also:—**bha e 'gar (aig ar) bualadh** i.e., "he
was at our striking", or shortly, "he was striking us". But
as the old woman said, "There's aye twa weys o' a thing",
and, to show the truth of this, we will bring our old friend
Seumas into the limelight again. Thus:—**tha Seumas 'gam
(aig mo) bhualadh** means that "James is present"—and
very actively too—"at my striking", i.e., "he is striking me",
but at the same time I am present, too—getting it in the neck,
so to speak—and I say:—**tha mi 'gam (aig mo) bhualadh**,
i.e., "I am (present) at my striking", in short "I am being
struck".

In the past time I would say:—**bha mi 'gam (aig mo)
bhualadh**, i.e., "I was at my striking", or "I was being
struck". So, too:—**bha iad 'gam (aig am) bualadh**, i.e.,
"they were at their striking", i.e., "they were being struck".
Compare the old Scots phrase:—"They were at their kirkin'
last Sawbath", or "they were being kirked."

In time to come—**bithidh mi 'gam (aig mo) bhualadh**,
i.e., "I will be at my striking", "I will be struck", and again:—
bhithinn 'gam (aig mo) bhualadh, i.e., "I would be at
my striking", or "I would be struck".

A common way of speaking in Glasgow, and perhaps in

other towns is to say, "I am after telling you", "he is after striking the man", etc., which mean, "I have told you", and "he has struck the man". In Gaelic this last example is:— **tha e air bualadh an duine** or **tha e air an duine a bhualadh,** and from this we can see that the little word **air,** which we know means "on", can also mean "after".

Compare the English phrase:—"On hearing the news he went to tell his friend", where "on" also means "after". Now, as we have said, **tha mi 'gam bhualadh** means "I am being struck", and so, too, **tha mi air mo bhualadh** means "I am after being struck" or "I have been struck"; **bha thu air do bhualadh,** "you were after being struck" or "you had been struck"; **bithidh e air a bhualadh,** "he will be after being struck" or "he will have been struck"; **bhitheadh iad air am bualadh** "they would be after being struck", or "they would have been struck".

VOCABULARY

brògan caola (brāw-kin kāīl-a), dress shoes.
call (kā-ool), losing.
crìochnachadh (krēēuch-nach-ugh), finishing.
dìg (jeek), ditch.
dòirteadh (dāwrst-ugh), pouring.
ítealan (āitsh-illan), an aeroplane.
fàgail (fāk-ul), leaving.
gu moch (gu māwch), early.
iongnadh (yōū-nugh), surprise.
milleadh (mēēl-yugh), destroying.
pàidheadh (pāh-yugh), paying.
sgrìobhadh (skrēēv-ugh), writing.
strì (stree), fight.
té, a "she"—a woman.
togail (tōk-ul), lifting, building.
tréigsinn (trāke-shing), jilting, deserting.
treòrachadh (trōr-achugh), guiding.

TRANSLATE INTO ENGLISH

Tha mi 'gam dhùsgadh. Bha e air a dhùsgadh.
Bhitheamaid air ar dùsgadh gu moch. Bha sinn air
tighinn. Tha a' chlach air a togail. Bithidh an litir
air a sgrìobhadh am màireach. Bha na tighean 'gan
togail. Cha n-eil longan 'gan togail a nis anns a' bhaile
so. Tha an t-airgiod a nis 'ga thrusadh. Bha an t-
ìtealan air a bhriseadh anns an strì.

TRANSLATE INTO GAELIC

They fell (were after falling) into the ditch. My dress
boots have been destroyed by the water. The house will be
built. You will be paid to-morrow. The book had been
finished. We were lost in the wood. She was jilted. You
were being guided home. We are being left without money.

SOLUTION OF LESSON 19

Bha iad air tuiteam anns an dìg. Tha mo bhrògan-
caola air am milleadh leis an uisge. Bithidh an tigh
air a thogail. Bithidh tu air do phàidheadh am màireach. Bha an leabhar air a chrìochnachadh. Bha sinn
air chall anns a' choille. Bha i air a tréigsinn. Bha
thu 'gad threòrachadh dachaidh. Tha sinn 'gar fàgail
gun airgiod.

Lesson No. 20

Is maith an naigheachd a bhi gun naigheachd. *No news is good news.*

Seumas has stood us in good stead up to this point as an example, but the reader will be shocked to learn of the tragic fate which has now befallen him, for he was foully done to death at the week-end by a mob of gangsters.

The "Press" briefly reported, **An uair a bha Seumas M—— a' tighinn dachaidh feasgar Di-sathuirne, bha e air a ghlacadh, air a bhualadh agus air a mharbhadh le mortairean**.

The heart-broken mother (the old lady wha aye had "twa weys o' a thing") told me of her sad loss in those words, **An uair a bha Seumas bochd a' tighinn dachaidh, ghlacadh, bhuaileadh agus mharbhadh e le mortairean**.

Thus, as you can see, there are two ways of saying that someone suffered something. The first, as shown in the last Lesson, is, **bha Seumas air a ghlacadh, air a bhualadh, agus air a mharbhadh**, which means that "James was seized, beaten and killed (by assassins)", and the second, **ghlacadh, bhuaileadh agus mharbhadh Seumas**, i.e., "seized, struck and killed was James".

Now this second way is got by taking the word of command, for instance, **glac !** (take !), aspirating its first letter and adding **-adh** to the end of the word, thus:—**ghlacadh e**, "he was captured". If the last vowel of the word is an **i** as in **buail !** (strike !) **-eadh** instead of **-adh** is added, thus:— **bhuaileadh e**, "he was struck".

Once again :—**dh'fhosgladh an t-searrag agus dh' òladh an t-uisge-beatha**, i.e., "the bottle was opened and

the whisky was drunk", where we see that, if the first letter
of the word is a vowel, or **f** followed by a vowel, **dh'** is put
in front. Compare Lesson 4.

If we want to say that the thing will be done in time to
come, we add **-ar** (or **-ear** after an **i**) to the word of command,
thus:—**fosglar** (short for **fosgailear**) **an t-searrag agus
òlar an t-uisge-beatha.**

There is a third way of saying that something is done to
a person or thing—and quite a snappy one, too—thus:—
bha Seumas glacte, buailte agus marbte, i.e., "James was
seized, struck and slain"

This form is got by taking the word of command and
adding **-te** to the end of it. Sometimes **-ta** is added, as the
spelling rule we gave in Lesson 11 might suggest, but to
add **-te** is the usual way.

Thus, too, **tha an dorus fosgailte, dùinte, briste,** etc.,
i.e., "the door is opened, closed, broken", etc. If, however,
we want to say that a thing used to be done, we do so by
adding **-adh** to the end of **glacte, dùinte, briste, fosgailte,**
etc., and aspirate the first letter of the word: thus, **ghlacteadh,**
e.g., **ghlacteadh an t-airgiod aig an dorus,** "the money
used to be taken at the door"; and **bhristeadh ar cridhean
le cion** (ky-ōōn) **airgid,** "our hearts used to be broken with
the want of money"

VOCABULARY

amar, canal.
amharus (āv-ras), doubt.
aonta (ōōn-ta), a vote.
bàth (bah), drown.
bàta-ola, oil tanker.
bràid (brātsh), collar.
ceud slat (kēē-ut slah-t), a hundred yards.
ceangal (kēh-ul), a tie; pl., **ceanglaichean** (kēh-leech-in).

cèarn (kyārn), a quarter, ward or district.

clò (klaw), home-spun cloth; pl., clòithean (klāw-yin).

Cuan nan Orc (kōō-un nan ork), the Outer Minch.

cuaran (kōō-ur-un), a slipper, shoe; pl., cuarain.

cunnt! (kōōnt), count!

earalaich! (ēr-al-eech), exhort!

fasgadan, umbrella.

foireann (fōr-ing), a crew.

fòmharach (fōvurach), a submarine.

Gearmailteach (gērm-ul-tshach), German.

gleidheil (glāy-ul), keeping, being held.

iomadh rud eile (ēēm-a rit-āīl-eh), many another thing.

làmhan (lāv-in), a glove; pl., làmhnan.

leighis! (lāy-ish), heal! cure!

lòdrach (lōt-rach), luggage.

lòinidh (lāw-nee), rheumatism.

margadh (marg-ugh), a market.

mèirleach (māy-ril-ach), a thief.

sàbhail! (sāvul), save!

Sasunn (sās-un), England.

seachad (shēch-ut), past.

taghadh (tāh-ugh), election.

tarag (tāruk), stud.

trannsa (trā-oon-sa), lobby.

turus, journey.

TRANSLATE INTO ENGLISH

Bhriseadh an uinneag an uair a bha mise a' dol seachad an dé. Chailleadh am fòmharach ann an Cuan nan Orc, ach bha na seòladairean air an sàbhaladh le foireann bàta-ola. Bithidh taghadh air a ghleidheil 'nar cèarn de'n bhaile (de'n bhaile, of the town) air Di-h-aoine agus bithidh na h-aontan air an cunntadh air Di-sathuirn. Reicear air a' mhargadh am màireach clòithean, bràidean, ceanglaichean, taragan, làmhnan,

cuarain, fasgadain agus iomadh rud eile. Air tighinn
do'n mhèirleach a mach o'n bhùth ghlacadh e leis na
h-earraidean.

TRANSLATE INTO GAELIC

The hammer was thrown a hundred yards. A German
aeroplane was lost on Saturday past on its journey to Germany
from England. Two boys were drowned in the canal last
night. My pencil was broken, and I could not write. The
luggage was left in the lobby.

SOLUTION OF LESSON 20

Thilgeadh an t-òrd ceud slat. Chailleadh ítealan
Gearmailteach air Di-sathuirn so chaidh air a thurus
do'n Ghearmailt o Shasunn. Bhàthadh dà bhalach anns
an amar oidhche an raoir. Bhriseadh mo chaolbhain
agus cha b' urrainn dhomh sgrìobhadh. Dh'fhàgadh
an lòdrach anns an trannsa.

Lesson No. 21

Cha n-eil fhios co is glice, am fear a chaomhnas no am fear a chaitheas. *The one who saves or the one who spends—which is the wiser no one knows.*

As poor Seumas has now shuffled off this mortal coil for good, we can safely say that, "he is as dead as a herring", or, in Gaelic, **tha Seumas bochd cho marbh ri sgadan**, where **cho** stands for the first "as" and **ri** for the second.

In case the reader has any doubt about the matter, we may add, **tha sin cho cinnteach ris a' bhàs**, i.e., "that's as shair as daith". Notice in this last sentence how **ri** has become **ris**; this happens before the word for "the" i.e. **an, am, a'**, or **na**. Thus, **tha an sgeul sin cho seann ris na cnocan**, i.e., "that story is as old as the hills".

Instead of using **ri** or **ris** for the second "as" we very often use **agus** (which means "and" as well), e.g., **tha e cho leisg agus a bha e riamh**, i.e., "he is as lazy as he ever was".

Again, "he ran as fast as his feet could carry him", becomes **ruith e cho luath agus a b' urrainn dà**. When we have a phrase after the second **as** with a doing-word in it, as, for instance, "was" and "could" in those examples above, we always put **agus** instead of **ri**.

In these days of poverty we are usually comparing our own luck—good or bad as it may be—with that of others. After a slice of good luck I may say, **tha mi cho sona ris an rìgh**, i.e., "I am as happy as the king"; but, if I should be extra well pleased with myself, I would very likely say, **tha mi na's sona na an rìgh** i.e., "I am more happy (happier) than the king".

In past time I would say, **bha mi na bu shona na an rìgh**, i.e., "I was more happy (happier) than the king".

In the same way, **tha e na's sine na mise**, i.e., "he is older than I am", or, in the past time, **bha e na bu shine na mise**, i.e., "he was older than I".

Now look carefully at those last two sentences; **sine** stands for "older", **sean** means "old", and the **na** which comes after it means "than"; **na's** stands for **na is**, which means "something or somebody that is", **na bu** means "something or somebody that was", so that the whole sentence, **tha e na's sine na mise**, really means "he is somebody that is older than I", and, in the past, "he was somebody that was older than I".

But the reader will say, "how do you get **sine** and **sona**? This we will now explain. In Lesson 9 when speaking of the "of" form of feminine or "she" words, we showed how an **i** was put into the word, and an **e** stuck on at the end, e.g., **bròg, bròige**.

Bearing this in mind and taking, let us say, **òg** meaning "young", we have **òige**, "younger". So also **glan**, clean; **glaine**, "cleaner"; **slàn**, "healthy"; **slàine**, "healthier", etc. But in Lesson 10 we saw that this **i** which we put into a word could make curious changes, e.g., **cas**, "a foot"; **coise**, "of a foot;" so we have **mall**, "slow;" **moille**, "slower", e.g., **tha esan dall ach tha ise na's doille**, "he is blind but she is blinder".

And again, just as **cearc**, "a hen", gives **circe**; so, too, **sean**, "old", gives **sine**, "older". **Grian**, "the sun" gave **gréine**, "of the sun", and so, too, **fial**, "liberal", gives **féile**, "more liberal"; **long**, "a ship", gave **luinge**, "of a ship", and hence **trom**, "heavy", gives **truime**, "heavier"; **creag**, "a rock", gave **creige** "of a rock", and so **deas**, "ready", gives **deise**, "readier"; **breug**, "a lie", gives **bréige**; and so, too, **geur** "sharp", gives **géire**; and **crìoch**, "an end", gave **crìche**, and so, too, **fior**, "true", gives **fire**, "truer".

But **sona**, like most other words which end in a vowel, is not changed.

Instead of saying that a person or thing is bigger, heavier, etc., than another, we may want to say that the person or thing is bigger or heavier than all else, i.e., the biggest, heaviest, etc.,

For example, **trom**, which, as we have seen, means "heavy", gave **na's truime**, which means "something that is heavier".

Now, in the sentence **tha Iain trom, tha Dòmhnull na's truime, ach is i Màiri as triume**, we see how "John is heavy, Donald is heavier, but 'tis she, Mary, that is the one that is heavier still".

As triume means "who (which or that) is heavier", and at the back of our mind we are comparing it with all else taken as a whole.

VOCABULARY

aotrom (āy-trum—ay as in "day"), light.

asal (āh-sul), an ass.

buailteach (bōō-ail-tshach), bungalow or summer-house.

càradh (kā-rah), plight, state.

ceò (kyāw), mist, fog.

daor (dāy-r), dear.

daoire (dāy-reh), dearer.

fuar (fōō-ar), cold.

fuaire (fōō-ar-eh), colder.

geamhradh (gyōw-rah), winter.

iosdan (ēē-us-tan), cottage.

leisg (lāysh-k), lazy.

leisge (lāy-sh-keh), lazier.

Lochlann, Scandinavia, Denmark.

mi-fhortanach (mee-ōrst-anach), unlucky, unfortunate.

seamrag (shēm-rak), a shamrock.

seasgair (shēsh-kur), comfortable.

'sam bith (sam-bē), in the world. (This is a short form of **anns am bith**, "in the world".) This translates the

English "at all": e.g., **rud 'sam bith**, "anything at all".
Thus **cha n-eil rud 'sam bith agam**, "I have
nothing at all, nothing in the world".

sgoth-chaol (skaw-chāīl), a yacht.
tapaidh (tāh-pee), clever.
tapaidhe, cleverer.
tiugh (tshu), thick.
truagh (trōō-ah), sad, pitiful.

TRANSLATE INTO ENGLISH

**Tha Lochlann na's fuaire na Alba anns a' gheamh-
radh ach cha n-eil i cho fliuch. Tha turus anns an
sguain na's daoire na turus anns a' ghluaistean. Tha
e na's leisge na bha e riamh. Bha an t-Seamrag na bu
luaithe na sgoth-chaol 'sam bith eile ach bha i anabarrach mi-fhortanach. Tha buailteach daor ach tha
e na's seasgaire na iosdan.**

TRANSLATE INTO GAELIC

His house is older than mine (i.e., my house). Mary was
younger than her brother. A razor is sharper than a knife.
Donald is cleverer than Mary, but Janet is the cleverest in
the school. An ass is slower than a horse.

SOLUTION OF LESSON 21

**Tha a thigh-sa na's sine na mo thigh-sa. Bha Màiri
na b' òige na a bràthair. Tha ealtuinn na's géire na sgian.
Tha Dòmhnull na's tapaidhe na Màiri, ach is i Sìne as
tapaidhe anns an sgoil. Tha asal na's moille na each.**

Lesson No. 22

Trod chàirdean is sìth nàimhdean, dà rud nach còir
feart a thoirt orra. *Friends quarrelling and enemies
agreeing—these are things of which one should take
no notice.*

When we are comparing persons or things in English we
often use two different words—for example, "that man is
bad but the other is worse". The same thing takes place
in Gaelic, and our phrase would run, **tha an duine sin olc,
ach tha am fear eile na's miosa.**

Here **olc** means "bad", and **miosa** (mēēsa) means
"worse".

Again **math**, as we know, means "good", and just as
in English we say "better" and not "gooder", so in Gaelic
we say **na's feàrr** (fyār), or, as it has now come to be written,
na's fheàrr (na shār) and not **na's maithe.**

If we want to say "the worst" we say **as miosa** (as mēēsa),
and "the best" is **as feàrr** (fyār). Thus, **tha Seumas math,
tha Màiri na's fheàrr, ach is e Peadair as fheàrr de'n
triùir** (trōō-ur), i.e., "James is good, Mary is better, but
'tis he, Peter, that is the best of the trio".

One or two others that the reader should know are :—
mór, "big"; **na's mò** (also **motha**), "bigger"; and **as mò**,
"the biggest"; **làidir** (lā-jir), "strong"; **na's treasa** (trāy-
sa), "stronger"; **as treasa,** "strongest". Any others that
crop up will be mentioned in the vocabulary.

We often hear people say, "he is the better (or the worse)
of it". Now this can be turned into Gaelic almost as it
stands—for instance, **feàrr** means "better" and **de** means
"of it", and putting the two together we get **feàirrde** (fyār-
jeh), "the better of it".

94

Notice in the spelling, how according to our old rule, an **i** is put in before **rr** to balance the **e** at the end.

Now **is feàirrde e** would mean "'tis the better of it he (is)", and if we want to say what it is that the person is the better of, we put the name of the thing at the end thus, **is feàirrde e an t-airgiod**, i.e., "he is the better of the money".

So, too, **is feàirrde thu sin** means "you are the better of that"; and, in past time, **b'fheàirrde** (byār-jeh) **thu sin**, "you were the better of that", with **thu** sometimes pronouced tu after the **-de** in **fheàirrde**.

Bu, as we know, aspirates the next word, and **fh**, as we know, is silent, so the **u** of **bu** is dropped before **e** for ease in speaking.

Just as we saw with the **f** of **feàrr** above, so **fheàirrde** is often written instead of **feàirrde**.

Once again, **miosa** when it has **de** added to it, gives **misde**, "the worse of it", and hence, **is misde e am fliuchadh a fhuair e**, i.e., "'tis the worse of it he is", viz., "the wetting that he got", i.e., "he is the worse of the wetting that he got".

One little point is worth noticing here before we go further. Take the phrase "there is a heavy tariff on Irish cattle". This is turned into Gaelic by **is mór an earghair air a' chrodh Eireannach**, i.e., "'tis heavy the tariff on Irish cattle".

Now if someone starts to speak of this tariff, we might say **tha e ag ràdh gur mór an earghair air a' chrodh Eireannach**, i.e., "he is saying that ('tis) great the tariff on Irish cattle".

What we do in a case like this is to drop the **is** and for "that" write **gur** instead of **gu'n** or **gu'm** as we usually do.

We could just as easily put it this way, **tha e ag ràdh gu'm bheil earghair mhór air a' chrodh Eireannach**, i.e., "he is saying that there is a heavy tariff on the Irish cattle".

And in the past time, too, it is just as we would expect, **bha e ag ràdh gu'm** (note, not **gur**) **bu mhór an earghair air a' chrodh Eireannach**, or, **bha e ag ràdh gu'n robh earghair mhór air a' chrodh Eireannach**.

VOCABULARY

àrd, high.

àirde (ār-jeh), higher, taller.

bùrn (boorn), water.

déideadh (jāy-tsheh), toothache.

fuil (foo-l—pronounced very quickly), blood.

geal (gyal), white.

gile (gyee-la), whiter.

gealach (gyā-lach), moon (fem.).

ioc-shlàint (ēē-uchk-laintsh), cure, balm.

teth (tsheh), hot, warm.

teotha (tshāw-a), hotter, warmer.

tighearna (tshee-urna), laird, lord.

tuath (too-a), tenantry, peasantry.

TRANSLATE INTO ENGLISH

Tha am fear sin na's treasa na am fear so. Is teotha fuil na bùrn. Is e Glascho am baile as mò ann an Alba. Is treasa tuath na tighearna. An uair a bha an duine sin tinn dh'fhalbh e do'n tigh-eiridinn ach cha b'fheàirrde e sin.

TRANSLATE INTO GAELIC

John is taller than James. James is the biggest man in the town. The sun is brighter than the moon. Hunger is bad but thirst is worse. He says that Donald is the strongest man in the town.

SOLUTION OF LESSON 22

Tha Iain na's àirde na Seumas, or, Is àirde Iain na Seumas. Is e Seumas am fear as motha anns a' bhaile. Is gile a' ghrian na a' ghealach, or, tha a' ghrian na's gile na a' ghealach. Is olc an t-acras ach is miosa am pathadh, or, tha an t-acras dona ach tha am pathadh na's miosa. Tha e ag ràdh gur e Dòmhnull am fear as treasa anns a' bhaile.

Lesson No. 23

Abair ach beag is abair gu maith e. *Say but little and say it well.*

We have already shown how to form the past time and the future time of doing or action words. A few of those words, about ten in number, do not keep to our rule. They are, however, very easily learned; in fact, we have had a number of them already.

English, French and German are far worse than Gaelic in this matter, for they have hundreds of such words. Now to take one of these.

A common one is **abair !** which means "say !" but "I said", as we know, is **thubhairt mi** (hōō-irtsh).

We can see that this is different from the rule we gave, which said that, to show past time, all we had to do was to aspirate the word of command, e.g., **bris !** means "break !" and **bhris mi,** "I broke".

Suppose now we want to ask a question with **thubhairt**, we say, **an do thubhairt mi ?** or, **an d'thubhairt mi ?** (un-dōō-irtsh), "did I say ?" This is more commonly spelled **an tubhairt**—when the first t is sounded as d after the n and so, too, **nach tubhairt (mi)** (nach dōō-irtsh (mi)).

" Did I not say ?" would be **nach d'thubhairt mi ?** to which the answer is either **cha d'thubhairt (mi)**, or **thubhairt (mi)**.

Now to return to **abair. An abair mi** means "will I say ?"; **nach abair mi ?** "will I not say ?" **cha n-abair mi**, "I will not say", but note carefully **their mi** (hāre) "I shall say" and not **abairidh mi** as we would expect.

In English we have two ways of telling that something is

98

happening. We may say, for instance, "the man runs", or "the man is running".

The second way is the one usually found in Gaelic, e.g., **tha e a' ruith**, "he is running"; "I write" would in the same manner be turned into **tha mi a' sgrìobhadh**, i.e., "I am (a)-writing"; "I smoke a cigarette" would be **tha mi a' bleoghadh cochlain**, i.e., "I am (a)-smoking of a cigarette". Notice the "of" form.

Now let us try another doing word. **Thig!** means "come!" e.g., **thig an so!** "come here!" Now note, **an tig** (not **thig**) **thu an so?** "will you come here?" To which the answer is either **cha tig**, "I will not come", or, **thig**, "I will come" (not **tigidh mi**).

Now, "I came" in Gaelic is **thàinig** (hān-ik) **mi**, but "did he come?" is **an do thàinig e?** or shortly, **an d'thàinig e?** (un dān-ik). "He did not come to the club" is **cha d'thàinig e do'n chròilean**. Again as in the case of **thubhairt, an d'thàinig** becomes **an tàinig** (un dan-ik) and **cha d'thàinig** becomes **cha tàinig** (cha dan-ik). (Cf. p. 107.)

Now a word that you will require to use often is "do!" which in Gaelic is **dèan!** (jēh-n); "will you do your lesson?" is **an dèan thu do cheacht?** and the answer to this is either **cha dèan (mi e)**, i.e., "I will not", or, **ni** (nee) (**mi e**), i.e., "I shall do (it)".

Now if we were speaking in past time we would say **rinn e a cheacht**, or, **cha do rinn e a cheacht** for "he did" or "he didn't do his lesson".

How often during the day do we use a phrase like "Look here, Jim", or "Come here, Mary"?

Now, to put those into Gaelic we say, **Seall** (shā-ool) **an so, a Sheumais**, and, **Thig an so, a Mhàiri.**

The **a** before Sheumais and **Mhàiri** is just the English **o**, i.e., in "O James", or "O Mary", and it aspirates the first letter of the word that comes after it.

If that word, however, is a "he" or masculine word, we use its "of" form, hence, **Sheumais**, but if it is a "she" word we make no change in the word, except for the aspiration we spoke about.

VOCABULARY

amharclann (āvark-lan), a theatre.
brindeal (breen-jal), a picture.
caladh (kā-la), harbour.
ceacht (kyecht), a lesson.
comh-labhairt (kaw-lāvurst), conference.
daonnan (dāy-nan), always.
fìrinn (fēē-ring), truth.
sìothchaint (shēēch-ainj), peace.
ùine (ōō-nye), time.

TRANSLATE INTO ENGLISH

An uair a thàinig am bàta do'n chaladh thill na seòladairean dachaidh. Mur an tig e an diugh, thig e am màireach. Ma thubhairt e sin, cha do dh'innis e an fhìrinn. Leugh mi anns a' phàipeir nach eil Mac-gille-mhaoil a' dol do Chomhlabhairt na Sìothchainte. Their an duine sin daonnan nach 'eil airgiod aige.

TRANSLATE INTO GAELIC

Did you come home last night, James ? I did, and I was very tired. Did he say that he was going to the theatre to-night ? He did not. Will you come with me to the club to-night ? I will not, for I have no time, I'm sorry. Did James do his lesson yesterday ? No, for he was sick. That man will do the work if you pay him well.

SOLUTION OF LESSON 23

An d'thàinig thu dachaidh an raoir a Sheumais?
Thàinig, agus bha mi glé sgìth. An d'thubhairt e gu'n
robh e a' dol do'n amharclann an nochd? Cha d'thubhairt. An tig thu leam do'n chròilean an nochd? Cha
tig, tha mi duilich, oir cha n-eil ùine agam. An do rinn
Seumas a cheacht an dé? Cha do rinn, oir bha e tinn.
Ni an duine sin an obair ma phàidheas tu e gu maith.

In Lesson 8 we said that when the doing word, e.g.
cluinnidh, ended in -dh, tu not thu was used after it; and
this is also what happens after -as (or -eas).

Lesson No. 24

Cha n-eil mi 'nam sgoilear 's cha n-àill leam a bhi
—mar a thubhairt am madadh ruadh ris a' mhadadh
allaidh. *I am no scholar and I don't want to be one—
as the fox said to the wolf.*

At the present time the world is very much concerned with
"Debt". Now the word for this in Gaelic is **fiach** (fēē-uch).
If the debt is a big one we say, **fiach mór**, and, as the trouble
is more or less common to us all, unfortunately, we say,
fiachan (fēē-uch-an) **móra**, i.e., "heavy debts".

Notice that when one debt was spoken of we said **mór**
but in speaking of many, we said **móra**. So that when we
spoke of more than one, we added an **a** (not **an**) at the end
of the word **mór**.

" All countries, big and small", i.e., **tìrean móra agus
tìrean beaga**, are just as badly off.

Now the man who owns a little property and is deep in
debt has often to give a mortgage (**geall**), and if several of
his friends are in like trouble, they have all got to face **gill
mhóra**, i.e., "heavy mortgages".

Here we wrote **mhóra** instead of **móra** because the last
vowel of **gill** was an **i**—and this is what usually happens;
for example, **balaich bheaga** (not **beaga**), "little boys",
and further, **fear glic**, i.e., "a shrewd man", and **fir ghlice**,
"shrewd men". We put an **e** at the end of **glic** and not an
a, owing to the old Gaelic spelling rule which we gave in
Lesson 11.

Some boys have the knack of getting into trouble and of
hurting themselves in the process.

One "big boy" (**balach mór**) of our acquaintance fell

down the stairs and broke his leg. The news went round, and everybody was asking, **ciod e a thachair do'n bhalach mhór ?** And the answer was, **tha cas a' bhalaich mhóir briste.**

In these last two examples you will notice how **mór** has been aspirated. This happens when a little phrase such as, "to the", "from the", "with the", "by the", "on the", etc. (also "of the" in the case of "he" words only), comes before the name word (in this case **bhalaich**).

Suppose now that the accident befell his sister, then the people would say, **ciod e a thachair do'n chaileig bhàin ?** And the answer would be, **tha cas na caileige bàine briste.**

Caileag, as you may know, is a "she" word, and to get the "of" form of it, we not only put in an **i**, but fix on an **e** at the end as well, just the same as we did with **bròg, bròige,** and sometimes making a change, such as in **cearc, circe,** and **creag, creige.**

Now **bàn,** which goes along with the "she" word, **caileag,** makes exactly the same changes: thus **bàn, bàine.** Had the word been **mór** instead of **bàn,** we would have had **móire,** and in the same way **beag** would have become **bige.**

Now we will explain the first phrase, **do 'n chaileig bhàin.** You will remember how we said in a past lesson **sàil na bròige** for "the heel of the shoe", but **air a' bhròig** for "on the shoe", where we dropped the **e** but still kept the **i.** In the same way we drop the **e** at the end of **caileige bàine** and aspirate the first letter of each word because they come after a phrase such as "to the", "from the", "of the", "on the", "with the", etc.

Let us suppose, however, that a serious accident took place and many folks got their legs broken, then we should say, **tha casan nan daoine bochda briste,** or, **tha casan nan caileagan bàna briste,** or, again, **tha casan nam balach bochda briste.** In this last example we have used **balach** instead of **balaich,** i.e., the form of the word for one person rather than the form for more than one person. This

is often found in cases where the name word does not add
-an to make its plural

VOCABULARY

Art (ārst), Arthur.
anns am bheil, in which there is.
ball (bāhl-), a member; (pl.), **buill**.
bàta (bā-ta), boat; **bàtaichean** (bāh-teech-in), boats.
beann (byā-oon), a mountain.
beartas (byārstus), riches.
bòidheach (bōy-ach), beautiful.
cinntinn (kēēn-tshing), growing.
ciste (kēēsh-tye), a chest.
cruinn (krōōing), round.
dall, blind; **doille**, more blind, blinder.
gàradh (gār-ugh), a garden.
gun (gōōn), without.
gorm (gōr-um), blue.
mar, as.
màla, a bag.
mìn (mēē-n), delicate, fine.
nead (nyāte), a nest; **nid** (nyēēt), nests.
peighinn (pāy-inn), a penny.
ridir (rēē-tshir), a knight.
slàinte (slāntshy), health.
sruthan (srōōh-an), a stream.
ùr (ōōr), new; (pl.) **ùra** (ōōr-a).

TRANSLATE INTO ENGLISH

Casan nam balach móra.   Air na bàtaichean mòra.
Ri taobh an t-sruthain bhig.   Air an t-sràid fhluich.
An t-each bàn agus na h-eich bhàna.   Thàinig an duine
leis a' chù mhór.   Thubhairt an duine bochd do'n duine

bheartach, "Tha agadsa beartas, ach tha agamsa mo shlàinte". "Tha moran nid anns a' chraoibh mhóir a tha ag cinntinn 'nar gàradh. Choisinn mo mhac beag mar dhuais anns an sgoil, leabhar bòidheach anns am bheil sgeulan air Rìgh Art agus air Ridirean a' Bhùird Chruinn air an sgrìobhadh. Buill ùra air an deanamh an so.

TRANSLATE INTO GAELIC

Dark youths. On the fast trains. On the top of the high hills. The blue eyes of the gentle girl. The sails of the big ship. He gave a penny to the blind man. What is in that big chest? There are many men without work in the big towns to-day. The little boy's books are in his bag.

SOLUTION OF LESSON 24

Gillean dubha. Air na sguainean luatha. Air mullach nam beann àrda. Sùilean gorma na caileige mìne. Siùil na luinge móire. Thug e sgillinn do'n duine dhall. Ciod e a tha anns a' chiste mhóir sin? Tha móran dhaoine gun obair anns na bailtean móra an diugh. Tha leabhraichean a' bhalaich bhig 'na mhàla.

Lesson No. 25

Beatha Chonain am measg nan deamhan—ma's olc
dhomh cha n- fheàrr dhaibh. *Conan's life among the
demons—if it is bad for me it is no better for them.*

In the last lesson we saw how the little boy and girl of whom
we were speaking, had quite a chapter of accidents all to
themselves, but indeed those accidents might have happened
to anyone.

Now, **am balach mór** means, as we know, "the big boy",
and "the misfortunes of the big boy"—**tubaistean** (tōōpisht-
in) **a' bhalaich mhóir**—not **na tubaistean**, by the way, for
the first "the" of such phrases is never translated; but again
"the misfortunes of a big boy" are simply **tubaistean balaich
mhóir**.

However, had there been more than one boy, we would
have said either **tubaistean nam balach móra**, i.e., "the
misfortunes of the big boys", or **tubaistean bhalach móra**,
i.e., "the misfortunes of big boys".

Notice in this last phrase how the **b** of **balach**, which
means "of boys", is aspirated; this always happens when
nan or **nam** does not come before the name-word.

So, too, "the rifles of the young soldiers" is in Gaelic
isnichean (ēēsh-nich-in) **nan saighdearan òga**, but, on
the other hand, **isnichean shaighdearan òga** means "the
rifles of young soldiers", or, shortly, "young soldiers'
rifles".

Each of these young soldiers would, no doubt, unless we
are very much mistaken, have a **caileag bhàn** ("a fair-haired
lass") in his eye, so he might speak of **gràdh** (grā-ugh) **na
caileige bàine**, i.e., "the love of the fair-haired lassie", or
gràdh caileige bàine i.e., "the love of a fair-haired lassie";

but, of course, there is more than one fair-haired lassie in the world, so we may also speak of **gràdh nan caileagan bàna** or **gràdh chaileagan bàna**, i.e., "the love of the fair-haired lassies", or "the love of fair-haired lassies".

And a word to finish off: if we want to say, "on a big boy", we put it in this way, **air balach mór**, where we don't aspirate at all, although "on the big boy" would be **air a' bhalach mhór**.

Let us take **clach**, "a stone", which is a "she" word in Gaelic. **Tha an cù 'na shuidhe air a' chloich mhóir**, i.e., "the dog is sitting on the big stone", but, **tha an cù 'na shuidhe air cloich mhóir**, i.e., "the dog is sitting on a big stone".

Notice in this last phrase how when there is no "the" it is only the **mhóir** that is aspirated.

By the way when Christmas (**Àm na Nollaig**, i.e., "Christmas time") is coming near, we need to know the words for giving and getting "presents".

Suppose I say, "I gave a present to my friend", I put it thus, **thug mi tìodhlac** (tshēē-lak) **do m' charaid**, while he would say "I got a present", i.e., **fhuair mi tìodhlac**.

A cautious man might ask me, "did he give you one in return?" i.e., **an do thug**, or shortly, **an tug** (un-dook) **e dhuit rud-eiginn air a shon?** and I would reply either **thug** or **cha tug** (cha-dook), which is short for **cha do thug**. (Cf. pp. 98, 99.)

Of course, I might say **fhuair mi tìodhlac** or **cha d' fhuair mi tìodhlac**.

But perhaps our canny friend might have said "will you get anything?" i.e., **am faigh thu dad?** to which I reply, hopefully, **gheibh** (yo—pronounced very short) or, disappointedly, **cha n-fhaigh** (ha-nȳ).

My little son, however, has been listening in and remarks a bit anxiously, "will you give me a bicycle?" i.e., **an toir thu dhomh rothair?** If the "touching" affection of my friends doesn't altogether "skin" me, I shall say, **bheir** (vare)

mi dhuit rothair math, but if I am "fleeced", I shall have
to reply cha toir mi rothair dhuit idir, i.e., "I won't give
you a bicycle at all".

But let Christmas come, and if the bicycle does not arrive,
the young hopeful will go a step further and say, thoir dhomh
rothair, to which I will tartly reply, faigh dhomh an t-
airgiod, i.e., "Get me the money".

VOCABULARY

ail (ā-eel), a stamp.
an uiridh (un-ōōry), last year.
balla, a wall.
bun (boon—very short), bottom, foot.
cam, caime, crooked.
cuairsgean (kōō-arskin), an envelope.
deireadh (jāy-rugh), end.
dealbhte (jāluv-tshe), painted, carved.
feannag (fyān-uk), a crow, rook.
lorg (lōr-uk), a trace.
mall (moille), slow.
mur, unless.
tigh-òsda, an inn.
seachduinn (shāchk-ing), a week.
pailteas (pālt-shis), plenty.
poll (pole), a puddle.
uaibhreach (ōō-ive-ruch), proud.
ugh (ōōh), an egg; pl., uighean (ōō-een).
ùnnsa (ōōn-sa), an ounce.

TRANSLATE INTO ENGLISH

Air mullach nam beann àrda. Càrn chlach móra.
Le slait mhóir. An d'fhuair thu an litir a dh'fhàg mi leis
a' chléireach ? Fhuair, agus pàidhidh sinn na fiachan
sin aig deireadh na seachduinn. A Mhàiri, an toir thu

dhomh cuairsgean agus ail ? Bheir mi dhuit ail, ach tha mi duilich nach eil cuairsgean agam. An d' fhuair na balaich na h-uighean ann an nid nam feannagan air mullach na craoibhe àirde ? Fhuair. Is i bean duine bheartaich agus tha i ro-uaibhreach.

TRANSLATE INTO GAELIC

At the foot of the high tree. At the head of the crooked street. On a little table. We came home by a slow train. At the end of the Great War the soldiers returned home. There was plenty of trout in that loch last year. They saw the trace of a big foot in the garden.

SOLUTION OF LESSON 25

Àig bun na craoibhe àirde. Aig ceann na sràide caime. Air bòrd beag. Thàinig sinn dachaidh le sguain mhoill. Aig crìoch a' Chogaidh Mhóir thill na saighdearan dachaidh. Bha pailteas bhreac anns an loch sin an uraidh. Chunnaic iad lorg coise móire anns a' ghàradh.

Lesson No. 26

Is mairg a théid do'n tràigh 's na h-eòin fhéin 'ga tréigsinn. *It is a pity for the one who goes to the shore when the very birds are deserting it.*

"I went to the theatre last night", I said to my brother, or in Gaelic, **chaidh mi do'n amharclann an raoir. An deachaidh** (jēchy)? asked my brother. The words **an deachaidh** are short for **an do chaidh**, and mean "did you (thu) go?" **Chaidh**, "I went", I reply, but **cha deachaidh** (i.e., **cha do chaidh**) **mo charaid leam**, i.e., "my friend did not go with me".

Nach deachaidh? i.e., "did he not go", replies my brother, **théid** (haytsh) **sinn an sin còmhla oidhche Di-sathuirne**, i.e., "we will go on Saturday", is my answer.

But as I am fond of company and my brother is short of funds I say to him, **an téid** (un-jāytsh) **thu cuideachd, ma phàidheas mise?** i.e., "will you go, too, if I pay?" But he is a little proud, and replies, **cha téid**, I will not go".

C'arson nach téid thu? i.e., "why will you not go?" I persist. **Rachainn** (rāching), i.e., "I would go", he says, **agus dithis** (jēē-ish) **eile mar rium**, i.e., "and two others would go along with me", **ach cha n-eil sgillinn againn**, "but we haven't a cent".

Thachair tubaist dhomh an uair a bha mi 'nam ghluaistean, i.e., "an accident happened to me when I was in my car", a traveller said the other day.

An do ràinig thu Dùn-Éideann gu sàbhailte? i.e., "did you reach Edinburgh safely?" he was asked. **Cha do ràinig anns a' ghluaistean, ach ràinig mi leis an sguain**, i.e., "I didn't reach it with the car, but I did reach it with the train".

Cha ruig mi an t-Oban Lathurnach (lā-urn-ach) **an nochd**, i.e., "I will not reach Oban (literally the Lorne Oban—the Oban in Lorne) to-night", continued the commercial, **ach ruigidh mi feasgar am màireach**, i.e., "but I will reach it to-morrow evening".

Theagamh (hāik-a, perhaps) **gu'n ruig thu Sruighlea an nochd**, i.e., "perhaps you will reach Stirling to-night", said the other hopefully. **Tha mi cinnteach gu'n ruiginn mur . . .**, i.e., "I am certain that I would unless . . .", replies the traveller.

We have already shown how **le**, which means "with", when put before **mi** (me) becomes **leam**, i.e., "with me",

The same thing happens in the case of a number of other little words, e.g., **roimh** (roy) "before" which when joined with **mi** becomes **romham** (rāw-um), joined with **tu** becomes **romhad** (rāw-ut)—note the **d** where you might have expected **t**—joined with **sinn** becomes **romhainn** (rāw-ing), with **sibh** becomes **romhaibh** (rāw-iv).

But now notice how **roimh** with **e** (he) becomes **roimhe** (rāw-eh), with **i** (she) takes the curious form **roimpe** (rōimp-eh) and with **iad** (they), **rompa**.

Thus we say, **choisich e romhainn, romhad, roimpe**, etc., i.e., "he walked before us, before you, before her", etc.

In the same way we join **troimh** (troy) "through" with **mi, tu, e, i, sinn** etc., and we just get the same forms as with **roimh**, except, of course, that the first letter is always **t**, thus **tromham, tromhad, troimhe**, etc.

Take again **fo** which means "under". Now we likewise get much the same as with **roimh**, thus, **fodham, fothad, fodhainn, fodhaibh**, but with **e** (he) we get **fodha** (not **foidhe**) and with **i** (she) **foipe**, and with **iad, fopa**.

VOCABULARY

àros-dannsaidh (ah-ros-dā-oon-sugh), Palais de Danse, Plaza.

a' rùdhrach (rōō-rach), searching.

An t-Suain (un-tōō-a-ing—pronounced very short), Sweden.

chuir me, thu, e, etc., **seachad** "I, you, he", etc., "put past", i.e., "spent".

cluichean-gheamhraidh (yōw-rugh), winter sports.

calma (kālm-a), brave, hardy.

gu dearbh (goo-jēr-uv), indeed, certainly.

gu sàbhailte (sāv-ultsheh), safely.

Gàidhealtachd (gail-tachk), Highlands.

mar rium, along with me; **mar riut,** along with you, etc.

riarach (rēē-ur-ach), an attendant.

ban-riarach, a female attendant.

tha mi 'n dòchas, I am in the hope; i.e., I hope.

trillsean (trēēl-shun), a torch.

TRANSLATE INTO ENGLISH

Romham ; fothad ; troimpe ; rompa. An uair a ràinig sinn an t-àros-dannsaidh ghabh an riarach ar còtaichean agus ar n-adan (hats). Rachamaid do'n t-Suain air son nan cluichean-gheamhraidh na'n robh an t-airgiod againn. An ruig an saighdear sin dachaidh gu sàbhailte ? Tha mi an dòchas gu'n ruig, oir is duine fìor chalma e. Nach d' ràinig iad an toiteach an àm ? Cha d'ràinig ; bha iad cóig mionaidean air dheireadh. Chaidh a' bhan-riarach romhainn le trillsean.

TRANSLATE INTO GAELIC

Before him; under him; through you; under her. Will you go with me to the Highlands if I pay ? I will, certainly. He was searching for (**air son**) his book and it was in his own pocket. The thief lifted the stone and put the money under it.

SOLUTION TO LESSON 26

Roimhe ; fodha ; tromhad ; foipe.   An téid thu leam do'n Ghàidhealtachd ma phàidheas mise?   Théid, gu dearbh.   Bha e a' rùdhrach air son a leabhair agus bha a 'na phòca féin.   Thog am mèirleach a' chlach agus chuir e an t-airgiod foipe.

Lesson No. 27

Am fear nach seall roimhe seallaidh e 'na dhéidh.
The one who does not look forward will look back.

At holiday time we shall be either seeing or hearing from our
friends. Now **chì mi** (chee mee) **mo chàirdean** means "I'll
see my friends", but if I feel any doubt about the matter,
then I may write and say, **am faic mi sibh ?** i.e., "shall I
see you" ? or I may even say, **nach haic mi sibh ?** i.e., "shall
I not see you" ? (Cf. p. 36.)

In due time the answer will come back either **cha n-fhaic**
(nàichk), i.e., "You shall not see (us)" or **chì**, i.e., "you shall
see (us)".

Speaking to someone about this joy in store, I may say
tha mi cinnteach gu'm faic mi mo chàirdean, i.e., "I
am certain that I shall see my friends", or, on the other hand,
if the joy is doomed not be to mine, **tha e coltach** (kòltach)
nach fhaic mi iad, i.e., "it is likely that I shall not see
them".

But since so many people are laid aside with colds and
'flu, it may happen that I shall have to write and say to my
friends, **chìthinn** (chēē-ing) **sibh ach tha slaodan orm**,
i.e., "I would see you, but I have the cold", and, in case they
should be anxious to know whether I saw my brother or not,
I shall write, **bha mi 'n dòchas gu'm faicinn mo bhràthair**,
i.e., "I hoped that I would see my brother", and **bha dùil**
(dōō-il) **aige gu'm faiceadh esan mise,** i.e., "he expected
that he would see me".

It is then quite easy "to see" in future time, and we have
already shown in Lesson 7 how "to see" in past time.

According to all politicians worthy of the name, we shall
be hearing good news sometime soon, or, in Gaelic, **cluinnidh**

(klōō-ing-eech) **sinn gu'm bi rudan na's fheàrr**, i.e., "we shall hear that things will be better".

But some Doubting Thomas in the company may say with the cynicism usual to such, **an cluinn (sinn**—generally omitted) **gu dearbh ?** i.e., "will we indeed ?" while "the man who is always right" will chime in with **cha chluinn**, i.e., "we won't hear (that things will be better)", and then, scratching his head reminiscently as memories of the past come back to him, he says **chuala mi an sgeul sin roimhe so**, i.e., "I have heard that tale before".

Disgusted with this sad lack of faith, I answer back at once, **O an cuala ?** i.e., "O, did you hear (that tale before) ?", while my staunch supporter soothes my ruffled feelings by saying **na toir feart** (na dor fyàrst) **air ; cha chuala e a leithid sin riamh roimhe**, i.e., "Never heed him (word for word—do not give heed to him); he never heard the like of that before".

But Thomas is not so easily suppressed, and he replies with heat, **tha mi cinnteach gu'n cuala mise, ach cha chuala tusa**, i.e., "I am sure that I did hear (that), but you didn't". Notice **tusa**, not **thusa**, after **chuala**.

At this stage a peace-loving soul in terror of the threatened political dispute, stops the discussion by saying to the nippy one, **bi thusa sàmhach ; chluinneadh tusa tuilleadh na'n abaireadh tu na's lugha**, i.e., "you be quiet; you would hear more if you said less".

A little phrase **mu thimchioll** means, word for word, "about around", or in ordinary English "round about". Now this word **mu** joins with **mi, tu**, etc., just the same as the other little words, **do, le**, etc., but, as Sir Walter Scott would say, "it gets whammilt", and is written **um** before **mi, tu,** etc.

Thus we have **umam** (ōō-mam), "about me"; **umad** (ōō-mat), "about you"; **umainn** (ōō-maing), "about us", and **umaibh** (ōō-miv), "about you".

When **um** (i.e., **mu**) is joined with **e**, "he", an i is put in, and so we get **uime** (ōō-eem-eh), "about him", and so also with **i**, "her", we get **uimpe** (ōō-eempa), "about her"—just like **roimpe**—but with **iad** "they", we get **umpa** (ōōmpa), "about them".

VOCABULARY

B' fheudar (bāy-tir) **dhomh, dhuit, dha**, etc., "I, you, he", etc., "had to . . .", e.g., **b' fheudar dhomh falbh**, I had to go.

clag-uaireadair (klak-oo-ar-utar), an alarm-clock.
Uaireadair is a time-piece (remember **uair**, an hour), a watch or clock. **Clag**, which comes from the same source as the English clang, means a bell.

co-dhiùbh (ko-yōū), at anyrate, however.

gille-doruis (gēēly-dōrish), a doorkeeper, attendant.

mu thimchioll, about it.
Mu thimchioll is used thus:—**mu thimchioll na firinn**, "concerning the truth"; **thubhairt e sud mu thimchioll**, "he said that about him (or it)". Here we really have **mu a thimchioll**, where **a** meaning "him" (or "it") is swallowed up by the **mu**. Again:—**thubhairt i sud m'a (mu a) timchioll**, "she said that about her", where the **a** meaning "her" is kept. Again: **thubhairt e sud mu thimchioll na daoine anns a' Pharlamaid**, "he said that about the men in (the) Parliament".

òran, a song; **òrain**, songs.

TRANSLATE INTO ENGLISH

Umainn; umpa; tromhad; aice; leatha. An uair a thig e dachaidh, cluinnidh sinn a sgeulan uile. Am faca tusa nach robh ail air an litir sin? Cha n-fhaca.

B' fheudar dhomhsa pàidheadh air a son co-dhiùbh. A réir coltais cha n-fhaca esan gu'n robh an gluaistean a' tighinn, agus tha e a nis marbh. Tha mi cinnteach gu'n cluinn sinn gu'm bheil a' bhrindeal a bha air chall, air fhaotainn.

TRANSLATE INTO GAELIC

About her; about you (**thu**); before us; before them; with him. Did you hear that there was a letter here for you ? I did not, but I will see the door-keeper just now about it. I heard a story about you. Where did you hear it ? In the club. If I should see him, I would be pleased. He said that I would hear Gaelic songs on the wireless on Friday evening.

SOLUTION OF LESSON 27

Uimpe ; umad ; romhainn ; rompa ; leis. An cuala tu gu'n robh litir an so air do shon ? Cha chuala, ach chì mi an gille-doruis (agus iarraidh mi) an ceart uair air a son. Chuala mi sgeul umad (or, mu d' thimchioll). C' àite an cuala tu e ? Anns a' chròilean. Na'm faicinn e bhithinn toilichte. Thubhairt e gu'n cluinninn òrain Ghàidhealach air an dìth-dhealg air feasgar Di-h-aoine.

Lesson No. 28

Is maith am buachaill an oidhche: bheir i dhachaidh
gach beathach is duine. *Night is a good shepherd : it
brings home every man and beast.*

A farmer friend of mine owns a greyhound, **mial-chù**
(mēē-ul-chōō—ch as in loch). One day, while we were
talking together, a hare **maigheach** (mȳ-uch) ran across the
field. The dog at once started after it and in less than a minute
caught it, **rug** (rook) **am mial-chù air a' mhaighich.**

Rug air means "bore on" or, simply, "caught".

Again, suppose two men were running and one caught
up on the other, we would say, **rug e air,** i.e., "he caught up
on him", or, simply, "he overtook him".

Now, to return to my farmer friend again. When he saw
the hare rise, he shouted to the dog, "catch her !" i.e., **beir
oirre !**

I was a bit doubtful about the matter, and I asked, **am
beir e air a' mhaighich ?** i.e., "will he catch the hare ?"
and my friend answered **beiridh** (bāir-eh) **e oirre, gu
cinnteach,** i.e., "he'll catch her, sure enough".

Rug, by the way, has another meaning, e.g., **rug i
mac,** i.e., "she bore a son"; **rugadh** (rōōk-ugh) **mi ann
an Alba,** i.e., "I was born in Scotland".

We have shown in past Lessons how little words such
as **aig,** at; **le,** with; **roimh,** before, etc., could be joined
with **mi, tu, sinn,** etc.

There are one or two other little words like these we have
spoken of, and now that you have got the hang of the thing
you will almost be able to make the joinings for yourself.

For instance, there is **as,** which means "out of", and **ann,**
which means "in", or "into".

Now **as** with **mi** becomes **asam** (āss-um), with **tu** it becomes **asad** (āss-ut), with **sinn, asainn** (āssing), with **sibh, asaibh** (āss-iv), but now notice **as** joined with **e** which means "he", is simply **as**—the **e** being dropped; when joined with **i**, "her," it becomes **aiste** (āsh-tshe) and when joined with **iad**, "they", **asta** (āsta).

Ann meaning "in", or "into" runs on much the same lines. Joined with **mi** we get **annam**, with **tu**, **annad**, with **sinn, annainn**, with **sibh, annaibh**, and like **as** when joined with **e** it becomes simply **ann**—the **e** of course being dropped.

Along with **i** "her", we get **innte** (ēēn-tshee) (not **annte**), and with **iad**, "they", **annta**.

You know how useful the little word "dis" is in English: for instance in "disarm", "disconnect", etc., it means "off" or "away".

Now, we have the same word in Gaelic, only we sometimes find it as **di** (jee) and sometimes as **de** (deh), e.g.:—

"He cut a bit off the stick", **gheàrr e crioman de'n bhata**; however, when we join **de** with **mi, tu**, etc., we keep to the old form **di**, but as in the case of **do** we aspirate the **d**.

Thus **di** joined with **mi** becomes **dhiom** (yeem), with **tu, dhiot** (yeet), with **sinn, dhinn** (yeeng), with **sibh, dhibh** (yeev).

And once again the three warriors: **di** along with **e** "he", becomes **dheth** (yeh), with **i** "she", **dhith** (ye), with **iad, dhiubh** (yōō).

VOCABULARY

a' bruidhinn (brōō-ing), speaking, talking.
aodach (ēh-dach), clothes, cloth.
baraill (bār-ill), a barrel.
cianail (kēē-an-ul), forlorn, desolate, deserted.
cibean-bhile (kēēp-in-vēēl-y), lip-stick.
cròdha (krāw-y), bold, brave.

deamhas (jāh-as), shears.
deur (jerr), a drop.
falamh (fāl-uv), empty.
goid ! (gēh-tsh), steal !
leig as ! (leek-as), let out ! let go !
làithean a dh'aom (gh-ēhm), the days that have passed, i.e., lang syne.
sgàthan (skā-un), a mirror.
subhlach (sōō-luch), liquor.
toirmeasgach (tōr-mish-gach), prohibitionist.
ubhal (ōō-ul), an apple
ùbhlan (ōō-lan), apples.

TRANSLATE INTO ENGLISH

Leig as mo làmh ! Dh' fhàg e aig seachd uairean; cha bheir mi air an nochd. An uair a dh' fhosgail i a màla thuit cibean-bhile agus sgàthan beag aiste. Am bheil am fear sin tapaidh ? Tha e daonnan a' bruidhinn, ach cha n-eil ann (in him) ach an t-amadan. "Tha na baraillean sin falamh—cha n-eil deur annta", thubhairt an toirmeasgach, an uair a dhòirt e an subhlach a mach asta. Tha an tìr sin cianail, oir cha n-eil daoine ann a nis, ach thàinig iomadh saighdear cròdha as anns na làithean a dh' aom.

TRANSLATE INTO GAELIC

He threw his wet coat off (him) when he came in. Catch that boy, for he was stealing (**ag goid**) apples out of the house. I have a purse, but there isn't money in it. The thief stole my watch, but the policeman caught him. She cut a bit off the cloth with the shears.

SOLUTION OF LESSON 28

Thilg e a chòta fliuch dheth an uair a thàinig e a steach. Beir air a' bhalach sin, oir bha e ag goid ùbhlan a mach as an tigh. Tha sporan agam ach cha n-eil airgiod ann. Ghoid am mèirleach m'uaireadair ach rug an t-earraid air. Gheàrr i crioman de'n chlò leis an deamhas.

Lesson No. 29

Cha leasachadh air droch obair latha a bhi fada gun
tòiseachadh. *Beginning late does not improve a bad
day's work.*

VOCABULARY

àirde (ār-tsheh), height.
fad, length.
leud (lāy-ut), breadth.
òirleach (ōr-lach), an inch; **òirlich**, inches.
soireag (sōy-ruck), vase.
stad (stat), a stop.
taireag (tār-ik), a drawer.
tiughad (tyōō-ut), thickness.

Before saying **slàn leibh** (good-bye) to my readers in
this, the last Lesson, I would like to touch on a few common
phrases which crop up in daily conversation. For instance,
in English we say, "what price is this book ?" but in Gaelic
ciod a' phrìs a tha air an leabhar so ? i.e., "what the
price that (or which) is on this book ?" To which the
answer may be **tasdan**, "shilling"; **leth-chrùn**, "half-a-
crown", etc . "I got the book for a shilling", would be **fhuair
mi an leabhar air son tasdain**, i.e.,' 'I got the book on
account of a shilling".

We speak of size and weight in much the same way. For
example, if the book were nine inches long, we would say,
tha an leabhar naoi òirlich air fhad, i.e., "the book is
nine inches on length". And should the breadth of the book
be five inches, we would say, **tha an leabhar cóig òirlich
air leud,** i.e., "the book is five inches on breadth". In the

same way in speaking of its thickness—**tha an leabhar trì òirlich air thiughad**, i.e., "the book is three inches on thickness". Likewise, **tha an leabhar leth-phunnd air chudthrom**, i.e., "the book is half a pound on weight". Height, too is spoken of in the same manner. "A table a yard high" is **bòrd slat air àirde**, i.e., "a table a yard on height".

Now consider the phrase, **tha am bòrd aig am bheil mi 'nam shuidhe slat air àirde**, i.e., "the table at which I am sitting is a yard high". We would naturally expect **tha am bòrd aig a tha mi 'nam shuidhe slat air àirde**, but when a little word such as **aig, air, do, anns, le**, etc. comes before the **a** (which means who, which, or that) the **a** is written **an** (or **am** before **b, f, m, p**), instead of **a**.

One other thing you must notice is that we always use the question form of the doing-word in such phrases. In present time we would say **aig am bheil mi 'nam shuidhe**. In past time we would write, **am bòrd aig an robh** (not **bha**) **mi 'nam shuidhe**, i.e., "the table at which I was sitting"; and in time to come, **am bòrd aig am bi** (not **bithidh**) **mi 'nam shuidhe**. Another example is, **an tigh anns an robh mi a' fuireach**, i.e., "the house in which I was staying".

Keeping in mind that we must use the question form in such phrases, you will easily understand the following:—**C'àite an do chuir thu an t-airgiod ?** i.e., "where did you put the money ?" **Sin agad an taireag anns an do chuir mi an t-airgiod**, i.e., "there you have the drawer in which I put the money". And also, **sin agad an taireag anns nach do chuir mi an t-airgiod**, i.e., "there you have the drawer in which I did not put the money". So, too, **an duine o'n d' fhuair mi na brògan**, i.e., "the man from whom I got the boots".

One little point to finish off, **tha e a' dol suas do'n t-seòmar** means "he is going up to the room", or, if he has to go downstairs, **tha e a' dol sìos** (shēē-us) **do'n t-seòmar**, i.e., "he is going down to the room". When he has arrived up in the room, we say—**tha e shuas** (hōō-as) **anns an t-**

seòmar, i.e., "he is up in the room", or if he is in the room downstairs, **tha e shìos** (hēē-us) **anns an t-seòmar,** i.e., "he is down in the room".

If we are in the room upstairs and hear him coming we say, **tha e a' tighinn a nìos** (nēē-us) **do'n t-seòmar,** i.e., "he is coming up (i.e., from below) to the room", and if we are in the downstairs room, we say, **tha e a' tighinn a nuas** (noo-as) **do'n t-seòmar,** i.e., "he is coming down (from above) to the room".

Now we have reached the end of our journey. The reader who has followed these lessons carefully will have a good grasp of the principles of our ancient language and needs little more now save to gather a vocabulary together.

This can be got by listening to Gaelic speakers wherever possible, and by reading simple books—the simpler the better to begin with. One good plan for those who are so minded is to take the Bible, especially the Gospels, and read the Gaelic and English versions together. We hope that simple books will be available in the near future.

Gaelic dictionaries are a little dear, but Macfarlane's Gaelic-English dictionary is quite useful and cheap.

You need not be disheartened if you don't manage to speak Gaelic with a Highland accent.

No sensible person would expect it of you any more than you would expect a Highlander to speak English with an English accent. There are, in truth, as many accents as there are individuals; the main thing is to make yourself understood in the language, and this is by no means so difficult as some people think.

Now to let you into a great secret—Seumas's last words were, "Aye keep ca'in awa' !"

VOCABULARY CHECK LIST

Gaelic—English

a who, which, that, 19
a chionn gu because, 65
a mach out, 65
a nall over, 65
a nis now, 11
a réir according to, 53, 62
a réir coltais in all likelihood, apparently, 72
a steach in, 69
Abair-Eadhain Aberdeen, 76
abhainn burn, stream, river, 20
abhlan wafer, 61
ach but, 11
acras hunger, appetite (**acrais** of hunger), 65
a' bleaghadh smoking, 53
a' bruidhinn speaking, talking, 119
a' dol going, a' going, 15
a' falbh going away, going, 48
a' fàs growing, 15
ag cadal sleeping, 15
ag càradh mending, 53
ag coiseachd walking, 16
ag creidsinn believing, 16
a' feitheamh waiting, 72
ag òl drinking, 16

a' rannsachadh searching for, 53
a' rùdhrach searching, 44, 112
a' ruith running, 11
a' seinn singing, 16
a' smocadh smoking, 53
a' snàmh swimming, 16
a' soirbheachadh prospering, doing well, 57
a' suidhe sitting, 16
a' tòiseachadh beginning, 65
a' trusadh gathering, 53
agus and, 16
aig at, 11
aig baile at home, 25
aig taobh by the side (of), 53
aighearach funny, 53
ail stamp (*n*), 108
air on, 11
air an làr on the ground, 33
air bòrd on board, 48
air dheireadh late, behind, 69
air maduinn in the morning, 69
air son for the sake (of), on account (of), 53
airgiod money, 29, 48 (**airgid** of money, 48)

àirde higher, taller, 96; height, 122

Alba Scotland, 57

Albannach Scot, Scottish, 57

am bliadhna this year, 53

am faod mi (thu, etc.) may I (you, etc.), 53

amadan fool (*n*), 65

amar canal, 87

amharclann theatre, 100

amharus doubt, 87

an àite in place of, instead of, 61

an aghaidh against, 48

an ceart uair just now (lit. the exact hour), 69

an dé yesterday, 16

an déidh after, 69

an d' fhuair? did you, (he, etc.) get?, 61

an diugh today, 16, this morning, 69

an làthair in presence of. 61

an nochd tonight, 16

an raoir last night, 16

an seo, an so here, 19

an sin there, then, 36

An t-Suain Sweden, 112

an uair a when, 27

an uiridh last year, 53, 108

anabarrach tip-top, ripping, 53

ann, anns in, into, 11, 25

anns am bheil in which there is, 104

anns an in the, 11

anns an abhainn in the burn, 20

anns a' mhaduinn in the morning, 29

aodach clothes, cloth, 119

aonta vote (*n*), 87

aotrom light, 92

aran bread, 11

aran-donn brown bread, 29

aran-milis pastry, 29

àrd high, 96

armailt army, 32

aroid table cloth, 65

àros-dannsaidh Palais de Danse, Plaza, 111

Art Arthur, 104

asal ass, 92

ath- next, 48

athair father, 20

b'fheudar dhomh (dhuit, dha, etc.) I (you, he, etc.) had to, 116

baile town, homestead, 25

balach boy, 20

balachan little fellow, 53

balbh dumb, 37

ball (*pl.* **buill**) member, 104

balla wall, 108

bàn fair-haired, white, 36

ban-riarach female attendant, 112

barail opinion (**baralach** of an opinion), 53

baraill barrel, 119

bas palm (of the hand), 44

bàta (*pl.* **bàtaichean**) boat, 104

bàta-ola oil tanker, 87

bàth drown, 87

beag little, small, 11

beagan ùine a little while, 53

bean wife, 29

bean-an-tighe housewife, 33

beann hill, 37; mountain, 104

beannaichte blessed, lucky, happy, 37

beàrr shave (v), 62

beart set (n), 57

beart dìth-dhealgach wireless set, 57

beartas riches, 104

bith be (verbal noun), 81

blas taste, 45

blàth warm, 11

bochd poor, 11

bodhar deaf, 37

bòidheach beautiful, 104

bonn-a-sè halfpenny, 69

bòrd table, 25

bradan salmon, 11

bràid collar, 87

bratach banner, flag, 48

bràthair brother, 20

breac trout, 16

brindeal picture, 100

bròg (pl. **brògan**) shoe, boot, 20

brògan caola dress shoes, 84

brùid brute, beast, 41

buail strike, 20

buailteach bungalow, summer-house, 92

bun bottom, foot, 108

buntata potato, 76

bùrn water, 96

caidil sleep, 41

caileag little girl, 53

caill lose, 20

càirdean friends, 33

caith spend, waste, 53

caladh harbour, 77, 100

call losing, 84

calma brave, hardy, 112

cam, caime crooked, more crooked, 108

caolbhain lead pencil, 69

càr tramcar, car, 33

c'ar son? why? 48

càradh plight, state, 92

caraid friend, 20

cas (pl. **casan**) foot, 25

casan footpath, way, 25

cat cat, 11

cè, uachdar cream, 57

cè reòidhte ice-cream, 57

ceacht lesson, 62, 100

ceangal (pl. **ceanglaichean**) tie (n), 87

ceann head, 20

ceapaire sandwich, 62

ceàrn quarter, ward, district, 88

ceàrr wrong, 37

ceart right, correct, 25

Ceilteach Celtic, 72

ceò mist, fog, 92

ceud nòt one hundred pounds (£100), 29

ceud slat (a) hundred yards, 87

chaidh passed, went, 33, 72

cheana already, 25

cho dona sin as bad (as) that, 57

chuir mi (**thu, e,** etc.) **seachad** I (you, he, etc.) spent, 112

chunnaic saw (*v*, past tense of **faic** see), 33

chuala heard, 57

cia mar a how, what way, 69

cianail forlorn, desolate, deserted, 119

cibean-bhile lip-stick, 119

ciod e sin? what is that? 33

cinnteach certain, sure, 16

cinntinn growing, 104

ciontach guilty, 62

cìr comb, 20

ciste chest, 104

clach stone (*n*), 37

cladach shore, 53

clag-uaireadair alarm-clock, 116

clagan bell, telephone bell, 62

clò (*pl.* **clòithean**) homespun cloth, 88

cloichead passport, 72

cluich play (*v*), 58; game, 81

cluichean-gheamhraidh winter sports, 112

cluinn hear, 41

cnoc hill, 48

có? who? 16

có leis whose? 29

cochlan (*pl.* **cochlain**) cigarette, 53

co-dhiùbh at any rate, however, 116

cofi coffee, 25

cogadh war, 45

coinneamh meeting, 29

coisiche pedestrian, 62

coisinn earn, win, gain, 29

coltach like, 69

comh-labhairt conference, 100

còmhnard flat, level, 25

còmhradh conversation, dialogue, chat, 37

copan cup, 20

còta coat, 11

craolachan, dìth-dhealg wireless, 57

creutair creature, 20

crìoch end (*n*), 37

criochnachadh finishing, 84

crìochnaich finish, 72

crioman piece, 45

cròdha bold, brave, 119

cròilean club (of people), 53

cruinn round, 25, 104

crùn crown, five shilling piece, 65

cù dog, 11

cuairsgean envelope, 108

Cuan nan Orc Outer Minch, 88

cuaran (*pl.* **cuarain**) slipper, shoe, 88

c'uin? when? 72

cunnt count, 88

cuspair subject; material, theme, 45

dachaidh home, 16

dad anything, 29

dall blind, 37, 104

dàna bold, cheeky, 'gallus', 37

daoire dearer, 92

daonnan always, 100

daor dear, 92

dath colour, 45
deagh good, excellent, 16
dealbh-chluich stage-play, 58
dealbhte painted, carved, 108
deamhas shears, 120
deantach agent, 72
déideadh toothache, 96
deireadh end, conclusion, 72, 108
deoch reòidhte iced drink, 58
deur drop (*n*), 120
dìg ditch, 84
dìol pay, 65
dìot bheag breakfast, 65
dìot mhór dinner, 65
dirich ascend, climb up, 48
dìth-dhealg, craolachan wireless, 57
doille blinder, 104
dòirt pour, pour out, spill, 25
dòirteadh pouring, 84
dona bad, 37
dornadh box (*v*), 58
dorus door, 11
dreuchdlann office, 65
droch bad, evil, 37
duais reward, pay, prize, 20
duais-sgrìob sweepstake, 30
dubh black, 11
duilich sad, sorry, 25
dùin close, shut, 20
duine man, 11
dùn castle, hillock, 11
dùnadh closing, 77
Dùn-Éideann Edinburgh, 77
dùsgadh waken, 77

e he (or a masc. object), 37
e féin, e fhéin himself, 62
each horse, 11
Eadailt Italy, 72
Eadailteach Italian (*n*), 62
ealtuinn razor, 62
earalaich exhort, 88
earraid policeman, 37
eile another, other, 48

fad length, 122
fada long, 33
fàg leave, 25
fàgail leaving, 84
faiche playing field, sports ground, 73
Faiche nan Ceilteach Celtic Park, 73
falamh empty, 120
falt hair, 48
fanachd stay, remain, 58
faotainn get, 58
fasgadan umbrella, 88
feannag crow, rook, 108
fear-an-tighe house-man, man of the house, 33
fearg anger, wrath, 20
feàrr better, 30
féill fair, church festival, feast, 45
feumaidh mi I must, 41
feusag whisker, 45
fios knowledge, 25
fìrinn truth, 100
fliuch wet, 11
foireann crew, 88
fòmharach submarine, 88
fo'n under the, 58

fosgail open, 26
Fraing France, 73
freagair answer, 26
fuaim sound (*n*), 53
fuaire colder, 92
fuar cold, 11, 92
fuil blood, 96

gabh take, accept, 26
Gàidhealtachd Highlands, 112
gann scarce, 53
gàradh garden, 53, 104
gasda good, excellent, 26
geal white, 96
gealach (*fem*) moon, 96
geall promise, 81
geamhradh winter, 92
Gearmailt Germany, 73
Gearmailteach German, 88
geartach excursion, 73
geur sharp, 26
gile whiter, 96
gille-doruis doorkeeper, attendant, 116
gionach greedy, 26
giustal sports, 73
glan clean, 77
glas grey, 12
glas lock (of a door), 45
glasruich vegetables, 41, 77
glé enough, sufficient, 26
gleachd wrestling, 58
gleidheil keeping, being held, 88
gleus tune, tune in, 58
gloine glass, 26
gloine beòir glass of beer, 58

gluaistean motor car, 62
gob beak, 48
goid steal, 120
gorm blue, 104
greim hold, grip (*n*), 48
greusaiche shoemaker, 48
grian sun, 48
  gréine of the sun
gu dearbh indeed, certainly, 112
gu h-olc badly, 65
gu moch early, 84
gu sàbhailte safely, 112
gu tinn unwell, badly, 33
gu'm bi (mi) that (I) shall be (etc.), 48
gun without, 104
gu'n do chaill e (i) that he (she) lost, 33
gu'n robh maith agad thank you, 65
gunna gun, 20
guth voice (**gutha**, of a voice), 53
guthan telephone (*n*), 62

i she (or a fem. object), 37
idir at all, 37
ioc-shlàint cure, balm, 96
iomadh many, 26
iomadh rud eile many another thing, 88
iomain golf, golfing, 58
iongnadh surprise, 84
iosdan cottage, 92
is e do bheatha you are welcome, 69
is feàrr leam I prefer, 58

ìsbean sausage, 62
ítealan aeroplane, 84
ith eat, 26

là (*pl.* **làithean**) day, 12, 26
là saor holiday, 54
lach bill, account, 65
laidhe lying, lying down, 33
làithean a dh'aom lang syne, 120
làithean saora holidays, 54
làmh, (*pl.* **làmhan**) hand, 20, 37
làmhan (*pl.* **làmhnan**) glove, 88
làr ground, 33
lasadain matches, 26
làthair near, present, 37
leabhar book, 20
leabharlann library, 53
leag knock down, 62
leanabh child, 48
leig as let out, let go, 120
leighis heal, cure, 88
leisg lazy, 26, 92
leisge lazier, 92
leithid like, 37
  a leithid like him
leth half, 73
leth-uair half hour, 73
leud breadth, 122
leugh read, 26
litir letter, 26
loch loch, 12
Lochlann Scandinavia, Denmark, 92
lòdrach luggage, 88
lòinidh rheumatism, 88

long ship, boat, 12
lorg trace (*n*), 108
luag doll, 77
luidhear chimney, 77

mac son, 12 (**am mac,** 16)
Màiri Mary, 12
màla bag (*n*), 104
mall slow, 16, 108
mar as, 104
mar rium along with me, 112
mar riut along with you, 112
mar sin in that way, 33
mar sin leatsa same with you, 69
mar so in this way, thus, 33
marbhphaisg shroud, 41
marbhphaisg ort! curse you!, 41
margadh market, 88
mas e do thoil e please (*lit.* if it is your will), 65
màthair mother, 20
meas-cheapairean fruit sandwiches, 65
mèirleach thief, 88
meud amount, size, weight, 48
mi-fhortanach unlucky, unfortunate, 92
mìle mile, 69
milleadh destroying, 84
mìn delicate, fine, 104
ministear minister, clergyman, 33
mìlsean sweets, sweetmeats, 26

mìos month (**mìosa**, of a month), 73
mi-thaingeil ungrateful, 41
modhail polite, 65
mol praise, 20
monadh moor, moorland, 30
mór great, big, 12
mu about, 69
mu thimchioll about it, 116
mullach top, 45
mur unless, 108
mùthadh change (money), 65

na that which, the thing which, 45
nach bi (mi) that (I) shall not be (etc.), 48
nàire shame, 65
nead (*pl.* **nid**) nest, 104
neo-chadalachd insomnia, 49

o chionn ghoirid a while ago, 37
oda race-course, 73
òg young, 12
oir for, because, 26
òirleach (*pl.* **òirlich**) inch, 122 ,
oisinn corner (*n*), 26
òran (*pl.* **òrain**) song, 41, 116

pàidheadh paying, 84
pailteas plenty, 108
pàipeir paper, 26
pàirc park, 26

paisde child, 26
peann pen, 20
peighinn penny, 104
piuthar sister, 20
pòca bag, wallet, pocket, 26
pòg kiss, 45
poll puddle, 108
posta postman, 26
preaban circus, 73

rathad mór road, highway, 37
reic sell, 81
riamh ever, 37
riarach attendant (*n*), 112
rib hair, 73
ridir knight, 104
rìgh king, 12
ris for, to, 73
ro very, too, 26
ro-dhaor too dear, 58
roimhe before, 37
rothaidhe cyclist, 49
rothaidheachd cycling, 49
rothar cycle, 49
ruisean lunch (**ruisein** of a lunch), 66

sabaid brawl, row, fight (*n*), 58
sàbhail save, 88
saighdear soldier, 20
˙saighead arrow (**saighde** of an arrow), 54
sàil heel, 20
salach dirty, 41
'sam bith in the world, at all, 92-3

saoghal world, 26
saoil think, 26
saor-dhuais pension, 26
Sasunn England, 88
se he (another form of **e**), 49
seachad past, 88
seachduinn week, 108
seamrag shamrock, 92
searmonachadh preach, 32
searrag bottle, 73
seasgair comfortable, 92
seo, so this, 16
seoladh direction, address, 26
Seumas James, 12
sgàil-bhothan shelter, 73
sgàthan mirror, 120
sgeul story (**sgeil** of a story), 54
sgian knife, 12
sgillin penny (Scots money), 69
sgìth tired, 81
sgoil school, 12
sgoth-chaol yacht, 93
sgrìobhadh writing, 84
sgrùdadh-comais means test, 58
sguab brush, sweep, 26
sguabair sweep, sweeper, 77
sin that (*dem. pron.*), 20
sìn hand over, 66
sìos down, 37
sìothchaint peace, 100
siùcar sugar, 26
slaightear rascal, 37
slàinte health, 104
slàn leat good bye, 70
slaodan cold (*n*), 62

slat rod, 45
sluagh people, crowd, 20
snodhach hair-restorer, 73
so, seo this, 16
soireag vase, 122
solus light, bright, 49
Spàinnt Spain, 73
spiorad spirit, 16
spioradan spirits, intoxicating liquors, 16
sporan purse, 12
sràid street, 41, 45
sraidheag cake, 66
sreath queue (**sreatha** of a queue), 62
sruthan stream, 104
stad stay, 81, stop (*n*), 122
stòl stool, 33
stri fight, 84
suathan rubber, 70
subhlach liquor, 120
sùgh donn brown soup, 77
sùil eye, 20

taghadh election, 88
taingeil grateful, thankful, 41
taireag drawer, 122
tannasg ghost, spirit, 16
taobh side, 37, 45
tapaidh clever, 93
tapaidhe cleverer, 93
tarag stud, 88
té woman, 84
teich flee, 81
teine fire, 12
teòm [the] dole (**teòma** of the dole), 58
teotha hotter, warmer, 96

VOCABULARY CHECK LIST

English—Gaelic

badly gu h-olc, 65
badly, unwell gu tinn, 33
banner, flag bratach, 48
barrel baraill, 119
be (*verbal noun*) bith, 81
beak gob, 48
beast, brute brùid, 41
beautiful bòidheach, 104
because a chionn gu, 65
because, for oir, 26
before roimhe, 37
begin tòisich, 73
beginning a' tòiseachadh, 65 ;
behind, late air dheireadh, 69
believing ag creidsinn, 16
bell, telephone bell clagan,
  62
better feàrr, 30
big mór, 12
bill, account lach, 65
black dubh, 11
blessed, lucky, happy beannaichte, 37
blind dall, 37, 104
blinder doille, 104
blood fuil, 96
blue gorm, 104
boat long, 12 ; bàta (*pl.* bàtaichean), 104
bold, brave cròdha, 119
bold, cheeky, 'gallus' dàna,
  37
book leabhar, 20
boot, shoe bròg, 20
bottle searrag, 73
bottom, foot bun, 108
box (*v*) dornadh, 58
boy balach, 20
brave, bold cròdha, 119

brave, hardy calma, 112
brawl, row, fight (*n*) sabaid,
  58
bread aran, 11
breadth leud, 122
breakfast dìot bheag, 65
brother bràthair, 20
brown bread aran-donn, 29
brown soup sùgh donn, 77
brush, sweep sguab, 26
brute, beast brùid, 41
bungalow, summer-house
  buailteach, 92
burn, stream abhainn, 20
busy, throng trang, 26
but ach, 11

cake sraidheag, 66
canal amar, 87
car, tramcar càr, 33
carved, painted dealbhte,
  108
castle dùn, 11
cat cat, 11
Celtic Ceilteach, 72
Celtic Park Faiche nan Ceilteach, 73
certain cinnteach, 16
certainly, indeed gu dearbh,
  112
change (**money**) mùthadh,
  65
chat, conversation, dialogue
  còmhradh, 37
cheeky, 'gallus', bold dàna,
  37
chest ciste, 104
child pàisde, 26 ; leanabh, 48

chimney luidhear, 77
chop toitean, 77
church festival, fair, feast
féill, 45
cigarette cochlan (*pl.* cochlain), 53
circus preaban, 73
clean glan, 77
clergyman, minister ministear, 33
clever tapaidh, 93
cleverer tapaidhe, 93
climb up, ascend dìrich, 48
close, shut dùin, 20
closing dùnadh, 77
cloth, clothes aodach, 119
club (of people) cròilean, 53
coat còta, 11
coffee cofi, 25
coffee-house tigh a' chofi, 33
cold (*a*) fuar, 11, 92
cold (*n*) slaodan, 62
colder fuaire, 92
collar bràid, 87
colour dath, 45
comb cìr, 20
come thig, 70
come upon, happen to meet
thachair air, 77
comfortable seasgair, 92
coming tighinn, 16
conclusion, end deireadh, 72
conference comh-labhairt,
100
conversation, dialogue,
chat còmhradh, 37
corner (*n*) oisinn, 26
correct, right ceart, 25
cottage iosdan, 92

count cunnt, 88
cream cè, uachdar, 57
creature creutair, 20
crew foireann, 88
crooked, more crooked
cam, caime, 108
crow, rook feannag, 108
crowd, people sluagh, 20
crown, five shilling piece
crùn, 65
cup copan, 20
cure, balm ioc-shlàint, 96
cure, heal leighis, 88
curse you! marbhphaisg ort!,
41
cycle rothar, 49
cycling rothaidheachd, 49
cyclist rothaidhe, 49

day là (*pl.* làithean), 12, 26
deaf bodhar, 37
dear daor, 92
[too] dear ro-dhaor, 58
dearer daoire, 92
delicate, fine mìn, 104
deserted, forlorn, desolate
cianail, 119
deserting, jilting tréigsinn, 84
desolate, deserted, forlorn
cianail, 119
destroying milleadh, 84
dialogue, chat, conversa-
tion còmhradh, 37
dinner dìot mhór, 65
direction, address seòladh, 26
dirty salach, 41
district, ward, quarter
cèarn, 88
ditch dìg, 84

do well, prosper soirbheachadh, 57

dog cù, 11

[the] dole (of the dole) teòm
(teòma), 58

doll luag, 77

door dorus, 11

doorkeeper, attendant
gille-doruis, 116

doubt amharus, 87

down sìos, 37

drawer taireag, 122

dress shoes brògan caola, 84

drop (n) deur, 120

drown bàth, 87

drinking ag òl, 16

dry tioram, 12

dumb balbh, 37

early gu moch, 84

earn, win, gain coisinn, 29

eat ith, 26

Edinburgh Dùn-Éideann, 77

egg ugh (pl. uighean), 62, 108

election taghadh, 88

empty falamh, 120

end, conclusion crioch, 37;
deireadh, 72, 108

England Sasunn, 88

enough, sufficient glé, 26

envelope cuairsgean, 108

ever riamh, 37

evil, bad droch, 37

excellent, good deagh, 16;
gasda, 26

excursion geartach, 73

exhort earalaich, 88

eye sùil, 20

fair, church festival, feast
féill, 45

fair-haired, white bàn, 36

fall tuit, 20

father athair, 20

feast, fair, church festival
féill, 45

fight, row, brawl (n) sabaid,
58; stri, 84

fine, delicate mìn, 104

finish crìochnaich, 72

finishing crìochnachadh, 84

fire teine, 12

flag, banner bratach, 48

flat, level còmhnard, 25

flee teich, 81

floor ùrlar, 20

fog, mist ceò, 92

fool (n) amadan, 65

foot cas (pl. casan), 25

foot, bottom bun, 108

footpath, way casan, 25

for, because oir, 26

for, to ris, 73

forlorn, desolate, deserted
cianail, 119

France Fraing, 73

friend caraid, 20

friends càirdean, 33

fruit sandwiches meas-
cheapairean, 65

funny aighearach, 53

gain, earn, win coisinn, 29

'gallus', bold, cheeky dàna,
37

game cluich, 81

garden gàradh, 53, 104

gather trusadh, 53
German Gearmailteach, 88
Germany Gearmailt, 73
get faotainn, 58
get, did (you, he, etc.) g . . . an d'fhuair?, 61
ghost, spirit tannasg, 16
give thoir, 66
glass gloine, 26
glass of beer gloine beòir, 58
glove làmhan (*pl.* làmhnan), 88
go, go away falbh, 48
going a'dol, 15
golf, golfing iomain, 58
good, excellent deagh, 16; gasda, 26
goodbye slàn leat, 70
grateful, thankful taingeil, 41
great, big mór, 12
greedy gionach, 26
grey glas, 12
grip (hold) (*n*) greim, 48
ground làr, 33; **on the ground** air an làr, 33
growing cinntinn, 104
growing a fàs, 15
guiding treòrachadh, 84
guilty ciontach, 62
gun gunna, 20

had to, I (you, he, etc.) h . . . b'fheudar dhomh (dhuit, dha, etc.), 116
hair falt, 48; rib, 73
hair-restorer snodhach, 73
half leth, 73
half hour leth-uair, 73
halfpenny bonn-a-sè, 69

hand, hands làmh làmhan, 20, 37
hand over sìn, 66
happy, blessed, lucky beannaichte, 37
harbour caladh, 77, 100
hardy, brave calma, 112
he (or a masc. object) e, 37
he se (another form of *e*), 49
head ceann, 20
heal, cure leighis, 88
health slàinte, 104
hear cluinn, 41
heard chuala, 57
heel sàil, 20
height àirde, 122
here an seo, an so, 19
high àrd, 96
higher, taller àirde, 96
Highlands Gàidhealtachd, 112
highway, road rathad mór, 37
hill beann, 37; cnoc, 48
hillock dùn, 11
himself e féin, e fhéin, 62
hold, grip (*n*) greim, 48
holiday là saor (*pl.* làithean, saora), 54
home dachaidh, 16
home-spun cloth clò (*pl.* clòithean), 88
homestead, town baile, 25
hope, I h . . . tha mi 'n dòchas, 112
horse each, 11
hospital, nursing home tigh-eiridinn, 77
hot, warm teth, 96

hotter, warmer teotha, 96
house tigh, 12
housewife bean-an-tighe, 33
how, what way cia mar a, 69
however, at any rate co-dhiùbh, 116
hundred yards ceud slat, 87
hunger, appetite acras, 65

ice-cream cè reòidhte, 57
iced drink deoch reòidhte, 58
ill, sick tinn, 20
in a steach, 69
in ann, anns, 11, 25
in all likelihood, apparently a réir coltais, 72
in the world, at all 'sam bith, 92-3
in which there is anns am bheil, 104
inch òirleach (*pl.* òirlich), 122
indeed, certainly gu dearbh, 112
inn tigh-òsda, 16, 108
insomnia neo-chadalachd, 49
instead of, in place of an àite, 61
Italian (*n*) Eadailteach, 62
Italy Eadailt, 72

James Seumas, 12
jilting, deserting tréigsinn, 84
journey turus, 45, 88
just now an ceart uair, 69

keeping, being held gleidheil, 88
king rìgh, 12
kiss pòg, 45
knife sgian, 12
knight ridir, 104
knowledge fios, 25
knock down leag, 62

laird, lord tighearna, 96
lang syne làithean a dh'aom, 120
last night an raoir, 16
last year an uiridh, 53, 108
late, behind air dheireadh, 69
lazier leisge, 92
lazy leisg, 26, 92
leave fàg, 25
leaving fàgail, 84
length fad, 122
lesson ceacht, 62, 100
let go, let out leig as, 120
letter litir, 26
level, flat còmhnard, 25
library leabharlann, 53
lifting, building togail, 84
light, bright solus, 49; (*in weight*) aotrom, 92
like coltach, 69
like leithid; **like him** a leithid, 37
lip-stick cibean-bhile, 119
liquor subhlach, 120
little, small beag, 11
little fellow balachan, 53
little girl caileag, 53
little while, a l . . . beagan ùine, 53
lobby trannsa, 88

loch loch, 12
lock (*of a door, etc.*) glas, 45
long fada, 33
lord, laird tighearna, 96
lose caill, 20
losing call, 84
lost, that he (she) l . . . gu'n do chaill e (i), 33
lucky, happy, blessed beannaichte, 37
luggage lòdrach, 88
lunch ruisean, 66
lying, lying down laidhe, 33

man duine, 11 (*also* **fear**)
man of the house fear-an-tighe, 33
many iomadh, 26
many another thing iomadh rud eile, 88
market margadh, 88
Mary Màiri, 12
matches lasadain, 26
material, theme, subject cuspair, 45
may I (you, etc.) am faod mi (thu, etc.), 53
means test sgrùdadh-comais, 58
meeting coinneamh, 29
member ball (*pl.* buill), 104
mend càradh, 53
mile mìle, 69
minister, clergyman ministear, 33
mirror sgàthan, 120
mist, fog ceò, 92
money airgiod, 29, 48

month mìos, 73
moon gealach (fem.), 96
moor, moorland monadh, 30
morning, in the m . . . anns a'mhaduinn, 29; air maduinn, 69
mother màthair, 20
motor car gluaistean, 62
mountain beann, 104
must, I m . . . feumaidh mi, 41

near, present làthair, 37
nest nead (*pl.* nid), 104
new ùr (*pl.* ùra), 49, 104
next ath–, 48
novel (*n*) ùirsgeul, 54
now a nis, 11
nursing home, hospital tigh-eiridinn, 77

occasion, time uair, 27
office dreuchdlann, 65
oil tanker bàta-ola, 87
on air, 11
on board air bòrd, 48
one hundred pounds (£100) ceud nòt, 29
open fosgail, 26
opinion barail, 53
other, another eile, 48
out a mach, 65
Outer Minch Cuan nan Orc, 88
ounce ùnnsa, 108
over thar, 37; a nall, 65

reward, pay, prize duais, 20
rheumatism lòinidh, 88
riches beartas, 104
right, correct ceart, 25
ripping, tip-top anabarrach, 53
road, highway rathad mór, 37
rod slat, 45
rook, crow feannag, 108
round cruinn, 25, 104
row, fight, brawl (n) sabaid, 58
rubber suathan, 70
run ruith, 11

sad, pitiful truagh, 93
sad, sorry duilich, 25
safely gu sàbhailte, 112
said thubhairt, 81
sake (of), for the s . . ., on account (of) air son, 53
salary, pay, wages tuaras-dal, 58
salmon bradan, 11
same with you mar sin leatsa, 69
sandwich ceapaire, 62
sausage ìsbean, 62
save sàbhail, 88
saw (v) chunnaic, 33
Scandinavia, Denmark Lochlann, 92
scarce gann, 53
school sgoil, 12
Scot, Scottish Albannach, 57
Scotland Alba, 57
search rùdhrach, 44, 112
search for rannsachadh, 53

sell reic, 81
seo, so this, 16
set (n) beart, 57
shame nàire, 65
shamrock seamrag, 92
sharp geur, 26
shave (v) beàrr, 62
she (or a fem. object) i, 37
she, woman té, 84
shears deamhas, 120
shelter sgàil-bhothan, 73
ship long, 12
shoe, boot bròg, 20; shoe, slipper cuaran (pl. cuarain), 88
shoemaker greusaiche, 48
shore cladach, 53
shroud marbhphaisg, 41
shut, close dùin, 20
sick, ill tinn, 20
side taobh, 37, 45
side (of), by the s . . . aig taobh, 53
sing seinn, 16
sister piuthar, 20
sit suidhe, 16
size, weight, amount meud, 48
sleep cadal, 15; caidil, 41
slipper, shoe cuaran (pl. cuarain), 88
slow mall, 16, 108
small beag, 11
smoke (v) (a pipe, etc.) bleaghadh, smocadh, 53
soldier saighdear, 20
son mac, 12
song òran (pl. òrain), 41, 116
sorry, sad duilich, 25

sound (*n*) fuaim, 53
Spain Spàinnt, 73
speak, talk bruidhinn, 119
spend, waste caith, 53
spent, I (you, he, etc.) s . . .
chuir me (thu, e, etc.),
seachad, 112
spill, pour, pour out dòirt, 25
spirit, ghost tannasg, 16
spirit spiorad, 16
spirits (intoxicating liquors)
spioradan, 16
sports giustal, 73
sports ground, playing field
faiche, 73
stage-play dealbh-chluich,
58
stamp (*n*) ail, 108
state, plight càradh, 92
stay, remain fanachd, 58
stay stad, 81
steal goid, 120
steamer toiteach, 77
stone (*n*) clach, 37
stool stòl, 33
stop (*n*) stad, 122
story (of a story) sgeul (sgeil),
54
stream sruthan, 104
street sràid, 41, 45
strike buail, 20
stud tarag, 88
subject, material, theme
cuspair, 45
submarine fòmharach, 88
sufficient, enough glé, 26
sugar siùcar, 26
summer-house, bungalow
buailteach, 92

sun grian, 48
sure cinnteach, 16
surprise iongnadh, 84
Sweden Ant-Suain, 112
sweep, sweeper sguabair, 77
sweepstake duais-sgrìob, 30
sweets, sweetmeats mìlsean, 26
swim snàmh, 16

table bòrd, 25
table cloth aroid, 65
take, accept gabh, 26
talk, speak bruidhinn, 119
taste blas, 45
tea tì, 26
telephone (*n*) guthan, 62
telephone bell clagan, 62
tenantry, peasantry tuath,
96
thank you gu'n robh maith
agad, 65
thankful, grateful taingeil,
41
that (*dem. pron.*) sin, 20
that, which, who a, 19
that I shall be gu'm bi mi, 48
that I shall not be nach bi
mi, 48
that which, the thing which
na, 45
theatre amharclann, 100
theme, subject, material
cuspair, 45
then, there an sin, 36
thick tiugh, 93
thickness tiughad, 122
thief mèirleach, 88

think saoil, 26
this seo, so, 16
this morning, today an
   diugh, 16, 69
this year am bliadhna, 53
three trì, 26
throw tilg, 20
thus, in this way mar so, 33
tie (n) ceangal (pl. ceanglaichean), 87
time, occasion uair, 27
time ùine, 100
tip-top, ripping anabarrach,
   53
tired sgith, 81
to, for ris, 73
today, this morning an
   diugh, 16, 69
tonight an nochd, 16
too, very ro-, 26
toothache déideadh, 96
top mullach, 45
torch trillsean, 112
town, homestead baile, 25
trace (n) lorg, 108
tramcar, car càr, 33
trout breac, 16
truth fìrinn, 100
tune, tune in gleus, 58

umbrella fasgadan, 88
under the fo'n, 58
unfortunate mi-fhortanach,
   92
ungrateful mi-thaingeil, 41
unless mur, 108
unlucky mi-fhortanach, 92
unwell, badly gu tinn, 33

vase soireag, 122
vegetables glasruich, 41, 77
very, too ro, 26
voice (of a voice) guth (gutha),
   53
vote (n) aonta, 87

wafer abhlan, 61
wages, pay, salary tuarasdal,
   58
wait feitheamh, 72
waken dùsgadh, 77
walking ag cóiseachd, 16
wall balla, 108
wallet pòca, 26
war cogadh, 45
ward, district, quarter,
   cèarn, 88
warm blàth, 11
warm, hot teth, 96
warmer, hotter teotha, 96
waste, spend caith, 53
water burn, 96
water uisge, 12
way, footpath casan, 25
way, in that w . . . mar sin,
   33
way, in this w . . ., thus
   mar so, 33
week seachduinn, 108
weight, amount, size meud,
   48
welcome, you are w . . . is e
   do bheatha, 69
well (n) tobar, 12
went, passed chaidh, 33, 72
wet fliuch, 11
what is that? ciod e sin? 33